TRAINING THE ROUGHSHOOTER'S DOG

By the same author:

GUNDOGS: TRAINING AND FIELD TRIALS

Training the Roughshooter's Dog

P. R. A. MOXON

First published in the UK in 1977 by Popular Dogs.
First published in 1994 by Swan Hill Press
an imprint of Airlife Publishing Ltd.

British Library Cataloguing in Publication Data
A catalogue record for this book
is available from the British Library

ISBN 1 85310 501 5

Printed in England by Livesey Ltd., Shrewsbury.

Swan Hill Press
an imprint of Airlife Publishing Ltd.
101 Longden Road, Shrewsbury SY3 9EB, England

For Olwyn and Timothy

Acknowledgements

My thanks to the editor, *Shooting Times and Country Magazine*, for permission to quote from my 'Gundogs' and 'Gundog Forum' articles which have appeared in that journal, and to my friend and colleague, Jack Davis, of Gowna Gundogs, Hanley William, near Tenbury Wells, Worcestershire, for the help he (and his dogs) gave me at a long photographic session when they acted as models, with great patience and fortitude, in order to provide suitable illustrations for this book. Nor must I forget Dave Parish, of Redditch, who taught me what little I know about photography, and who makes such a superb job of processing my films.

Contents

Illustrations

Unless otherwise acknowledged in this list, all the photographs are by the author

In the text

Author's Introduction

This book is offered as a simple and straightforward do-it-yourself manual for the average novice roughshooter who is desirous of training a gundog to assist him in his sport. In my opinion, far too many authors on the subject make everything seem very complicated and difficult, blinding their readers with science and confusing them with unnecessary technicalities. This mistake I have endeavoured to avoid without, I hope, going to the other extreme and making it all seem too easy.

I first conceived the idea for this book towards the end of Hitler's war, when roughshooting was extremely popular and 'pot-hunting' a virtual necessity, thanks to stringent meat rationing! Nothing helps to fill the gamebag – and consequently the pot – more effectively than a reasonably well-trained gundog, and so I set about writing a simplified, easily understood and assimilated treatise aimed specifically at helping the one-dog man to educate a canine all-rounder. The fruit of my labours first appeared in 1946 under the title, *Gundogs: Modern Methods of Training*, published by the Burlington Publishing Co. (1942) Ltd, and subsequently in revised form in the Shooting Times Library, published in two editions by Percival Marshall and Co. Ltd. It was well received by critics and the gundog-owning public, but eventually went out of print, largely as a result of the success of my second and far more comprehensive book, *Gundogs: Training and Field Trials*, first published by Popular Dogs Publishing Co. Ltd in 1952.

However, pressure was put upon me to revise, modernize and expand my original 'roughshooter's bible', as some readers had been kind enough to dub it, because of its simplicity and practical appeal to the novice roughshooter. The owner who wishes to learn how to train a dog without tears or frills, with no aspirations towards field trial competition nor any interest in the so-called 'finer points' of gundog education, appears to demand a primary textbook of this nature, though I am certain that many will become bitten by the bug and progress to greater things, once their appetites have been whetted by my present offering!

Another reason for re-hashing (if this is the right word!) my original brainchild is the current popularity of roughshooting by loners, as opposed to formal and driven-game shooting which has now become so expensive. Indeed, in this respect we are almost back to wartime conditions when hunting was for the pot as well as for pleasure and relaxation – practical economic escapism, if you like!

Above all, any sportsman worthy of the name should be a *conservationist and a humanitarian*, and do everything possible to ensure that no bird or beast he fires at goes away wounded. To this end, the services of a retrieving dog are essential, all the more so if it has been efficiently trained and is sensibly handled from the start.

I have had a lot of fun – and a lot more work than I had anticipated! – in modernizing and expanding this book, which I hope will inspire and assist roughshooters to acquire and educate a suitable puppy with the object of enhancing their sport and conserving game. I have included a chapter, in question-and-answer form, which deals with *some* of the most common problems encountered by novice owner-trainers (it would be quite impossible to cover them all), because this is something that I always sought, but never found, in the training manuals I read when I was a novice at the game. I have also endeavoured to illustrate with my own photographs many of the more important aspects of the basic training of a gundog for much the same reason. Although the models used are all English springer spaniels, the points illustrated are applicable to any breed of gundog.

As I wrote in 1946, it is my belief that there is a great future for the gundog and the roughshooter, and I hope that this volume may go some way towards helping the one to understand the other, which would not only increase the shooter's enjoyment of his sport, but would better the lot of many gundogs (so often sadly misunderstood) and result in that killing combination – the understanding handler and his clever dog.

PETER MOXON

Beoley Kennels, Redditch, Worcestershire, 1977

I

Selecting and training the puppy

CHOICE AND SELECTION

The average shooting man is often bewildered by the various claims put forward for the different breeds of gundog, and frequently ends up with a puppy from a breed which is totally unsuitable for the work in hand. Throughout this book I am assuming that the puppy we are training is going to be a maid-of-all-work for the shooting man, and will, in the course of time, be called upon not only to retrieve dead and wounded game but to quest for unshot game and rabbits, to remain steady to flush, to retrieve if anything is down, and to enter water upon command to retrieve dead or wounded birds thereon.

A great deal is expected of the present-day gundog, whatever his breed, and of course each man has his own preference. I have, in my time, trained spaniels, retrievers and pointers to become the shooter's handyman, and have had a good opportunity to decide in my own mind which breed has come off best. But for the sake of the novice I will deal in general terms with the main gundog breeds, so that he will be able to decide which breed will be most suitable for him.

The Labrador retriever is a very popular dog today, and can be seen at almost any shoot. He is excellent in water as a rule, tractable and easily handled, and a splendid companion for children. As a worker he is comparatively easily trained (if from a working strain, but more of this anon), and can be taught to quest like a spaniel. His disadvantages, from my point of view, are his size, which is a consideration if he is to live indoors and ride in the family car, and, from the point of view of hunting, when he is in dense cover; the fact that Labradors do not take *naturally* to spaniel work (hunting-up game); and finally the aversion of so many strains to really tough cover.

The Irish water spaniel and curly-coated retriever can be bracketed together for all practical purposes. I have found that these breeds need much more careful and prolonged training, being more stubborn and self-willed, than the other varieties of gundog. Their size and their coats are a disadvantage in cover, the latter picking up all sorts of burrs and brambles and while these dogs excel in water, they are not really suitable for use as general-purpose dogs.

Much the same may be said of golden and flat-coated retrievers which, though much more easily trained, are long in the leg and do not always adapt themselves to questing unshot game, though even for this work they have their champions.

Pointers and setters need hardly be seriously considered for general work for, while I am not gainsaying that they can be trained to become efficient all-rounders, they need a great deal of handling and their whole history is against their use in this capacity. The setter ranges too wide, and to curb him is to slow him to the point of pottering; the pointer's coat is so thin that it is almost cruel to work him in thick and thorny cover.

On the other hand, the German pointer-retriever breeds can and do make the most useful general-purpose gundogs if properly trained and experienced. These comparatively new breeds require rather specialized training and, I feel, are still not fully appreciated in this country because, up to the present, too little attention has been paid over here to finding the correct training technique for what are, when all is said and done, specialized all-rounders. The breed societies can offer help in this respect, and I suggest that anyone desirous of owning and working a 'German' should seek their aid.

There remain to be considered the spaniel breeds. I must confess to being a lover of all spaniels, particularly the English springer, of which breed I have had the greatest practical experience of all. Whilst clumber (becoming rare these days, and built too heavily for work), Sussex and field spaniels are all good dogs for general work, they have never yet made such headway in public favour (for work) as the English springer. The cocker spaniel is, of course, a very popular dog, but I fear that detrimental influences have resulted in the production of a breed of dog which, on the whole, is far too highly strung (often to the point of gun-shyness) and generally scatterbrained for work with the gun. This is much to be deplored, and a certain consolation may be found in the fact that there *are* strains which have not been so spoiled, but which have been kept for work instead of degenerating into pets. These strains are jealously guarded by their owners, and the average man will be hard put to find a really good-working cocker.

The English springer has long held pride of place in the spaniel world from a working point of view, and it is comparatively easy to obtain a puppy from a working strain. Springers vary in type to an amazing degree, ranging from little dogs no bigger than a cocker up to animals which run the setter very close as regards length of leg. This is not the place to discuss the merits or demerits of the different sizes of springer, but it should be borne in mind that, as a general rule, the real working and field trial strains are smaller than those favoured by the show bench fraternity, and that for general work a large dog is neither necessary nor desirable. I might here add that most of what has been written about the English springer applies equally to the Welsh springer spaniel, and there is really little to choose between the two breeds except that 'Welshmen' are not such good retrievers as the English. If anything the English springer is a much more natural retriever, but nowadays any spaniel puppy of working strain should take to retrieving without any elaborate lessons being necessary.

Whichever breed of gundog is finally selected for training, it cannot be too often or too strongly emphasized that *the puppy should be of working strain.* Many dishonest breeders and dealers will palm off almost anything as being of working stock, but the wise shooter will insist upon scrutinizing the pedigree of the puppy and, if this all-important document conveys nothing to him, taking it to a man who knows the breed and the various working strains. A puppy from a litter, the sire and the dam of which have been trained to the gun and work well, should prove easy to train and to handle. The progeny of non-working parents are often worse then useless. While field trials are (quite wrongly) derided in many quarters, they serve at least one useful purpose for the shooting man: the pedigree of a gundog which contains the names of a number of field trial winners and champions speaks highly for the puppy's prospects as a worker. No dog can win at a trial, far less become an F.T. champion, unless he is a good worker in practically every respect. The only quality in a dog which field trials cannot always reveal is the all-important one of stamina, but it can be assumed that few men would sink so low as to train a dog for trials if his stamina were in doubt, and one can frequently get a good idea about this if the parents of the puppy in question can be seen working. The man who is looking for a puppy for use in the field should not pay attention to the *show* bench history of the breed concerned, but rather concentrate upon the *working* history and record of the parents, grandparents and so on.

A few words upon the subject of inbreeding may not be amiss, for this is a matter which can create doubts and fears. The pedigree of a dog often shows a certain amount of inbreeding, but this is more often beneficial than otherwise. In no way other than by resorting to judicious inbreeding can the really important features of a strain or breed be retained. Too much inbreeding, certainly, is an evil thing, and here again the advice of an expert should be sought. It is only when inbreeding is conducted too much and with unhealthy specimens exhibiting the same fault that trouble ensues.

To sum up, for the man who is still undecided, I should unhesitatingly recommend a good springer spaniel of working strain. These dogs make perfect companions, being intelligent, docile, and easily trained both to the house and to the gun. A range of sizes is available, so that one can be chosen most suitable from this angle, and no trouble should be found in training the dog to hunt the roughest cover, enter water and retrieve all game. In many respects I believe the present-day working springer to be superior to every other breed of gundog, especially with regard to nose and general intelligence. Hard-mouthed specimens are rare, and a really well-trained springer is a pleasure to watch and to shoot over. Spaniels have for generations been used for finding and flushing unshot game and rabbits, and a natural aptitude for this work is displayed by all those of working strain, whereas retrievers often have to be *taught* to hunt-up game.

Lastly, but by no means least important, is the consideration that the springer is a hardy dog when kept in good condition, and will work better in extremes of climate than the retriever breeds. Because of this, springers are favoured on the grouse moors where the heat in August is often intense. I have had my spaniels working keenly on days when accompanying Labradors were all-in on account of the heat.

Another frequent question is, 'At what age should training begin?' The usual evasive answer given is, 'It all depends on the dog.' I will go a step further and say that it depends much more on the trainer! Do not attempt to teach too much too quickly. Be gentle in all your actions, and never cow the pup. Keep him bright and merry. If you cannot trust your temper, defer training until he is *at least* six to ten months old – or, better still, give up the idea of training altogether! The nature of the dog is much more important in connection with starting him on game work proper. A sober-minded dog can begin field work earlier than his more impetuous brother.

INTRODUCTION TO TRAINING

Over the years it has been brought home to me again and again that the average owner-trainer cheats himself – and his dog – by being over-impatient. He (or she) tends to skimp the all-important early hand training in eagerness to get the dog into the more interesting and practical field work. In other words, the tendency is to try to put an old head on young shoulders or, to use a very apt simile, to put the recruit into battle before it has had its full course of square-bashing.

No greater mistake could possibly be made. Serious gundog trainers are agreed that the preliminary obedience and hand training is by far the most important part of the job. Once a dog is under control half the battle is won, but to skimp early training (wherein there is comparatively little temptation for the dog) and then expect it to behave under exciting field conditions is simply asking the impossible and courting disaster. Remember that, in any gundog worthy of the name, hunting, facing cover and water and, to a large extent, retrieving are natural instincts which will quickly make themselves apparent. The unnatural aspect of training lies in teaching the dog to utilize its natural instincts to the advantage of its handler and not simply for its own gratification.

So, before embarking upon the training of his gundog puppy, and as a preliminary to reading the following pages, I implore my reader to put himself in the right frame of mind for both tasks!

Given the right canine material to start with (and this is essential to success), gundog training is *not* difficult if properly approached and conducted with consideration for the pupil. We humans are very apt to credit a dog with a reasoning power similar to ours – something which it just has not got. Everything a dog learns is by association of ideas and example. It can very easily be given totally the wrong impression which is difficult (if not impossible) to eradicate. One cannot explain to a dog, as to a child, where it has gone wrong, and for this reason I particularly commend to readers the section upon punishment.

The art (if this is the right word) of gundog training is the ability to assess the temperament of the individual pupil and to know where to stop. No two dogs are alike and, unless temperament is taken into consideration, success in training is unlikely. *The* most important characteristic of a gundog is, in my opinion, the will to please or what I term 'trainability', a term which explains itself. Puppies of the right strains bred from generations of working and field trial parents are likely to possess this in varying degrees. I like a dog which takes an interest in and watches me – really looks into my eyes with a kindly expression. Such a dog invariably trains easily and proves a joy to handle, but it is not always easy to pick out one from a litter of, say, eight weeks of age. But at six or eight months of age the task is easier and for this reason it is often advisable to defer the purchase of a puppy until one can be found that is obviously 'with' you and combines this charming characteristic with natural hunting and retrieving ability plus courage, pace and style. Quite a tall order!

I mentioned earlier that many novice trainers skimp early obedience training and fail to get their pupils thoroughly under control before embarking upon more advanced field work. On the other hand, I have known countless dogs ruined by over-enthusiasm on the part of their owner-trainers who so sicken and bore their dogs by over-doing the hand training that the unfortunate animals become spiritless and lose drive and all enthusiasm for work, ending up as uninteresting potterers who work because they have to instead of because they enjoy it. No! The trainer must retain a sense of proportion and keep the balance right, obtaining implicit obedience without in any way impairing drive and enthusiasm in his pupil. This is not as difficult as it may sound if he takes an intelligent interest in his dog and studies its temperament, not only when out training but at all times. Try to keep lessons enjoyable for the dog. As soon as it shows any signs of boredom or slackness, give it a rest, change the exercise or just let it have a good free-for-all.

RABBITS AND GAME

Although throughout this book the rabbit has been referred to as the main quarry and real-thing practice for the pupil, I realize that nowadays in many areas rabbits are harder to come by than game birds. This need not, however, cause consternation to the reader, for almost everything that has been written about training on rabbits can be applied equally to birds, although the temptation to chase a flying pheasant or covey of partridges will not be so great. For this reason, rabbits remain the ideal medium in which to give experience to the average roughshooter's dog (hares, too, for steadiness lessons), and in most districts there are still rabbits to be found, although not in such great numbers as formerly. This is probably not altogether a bad thing, for the roughshooter's dog comes into its own on ground where every head of game must be searched for and pushed out. On ground teeming with game the shooter can himself kick up enough game to keep his barrels warm! On the credit side, scarcity of game and rabbits can mean prolonging the training and experiencing of the pupil, thus preventing the tendency to get it along too quickly and achieving a greater degree of control in the end product.

THE CHECK CORD

The check cord is a very useful item of training equipment *if properly used at the right time on the right pupil*, but it should not be abused. Many trainers *never* use a check cord and certainly in the case of very dog-wise men and women it may be quite unnecessary. It can be a confounded nuisance on certain types of ground, and always has the disadvantage that an intelligent dog quickly learns that when it is wearing it the handler is on top and so behaves accordingly, but reacts quite differently the moment it is removed. I can go so far as to say that if the initial obedience work is given thoroughly the great majority of gundogs need never wear a check cord, even when commencing field work. I endeavour to keep it as a last resort but, for all that, it still provides the novice trainer with an extra long arm and, intelligently used, can have a very useful application in many stages of training. My advice is that the trainer should endeavour to educate his pupil without too much reliance on the check, retaining it for use on those occasions when it really appears to be necessary. If a dog can be got through its course of training without the cord, so much the better, but throughout this book I have suggested its use in those circumstances where it *may* be necessary. This should not be taken to mean that it *must* be used.

Nowadays, thanks to modern science, it is possible to use a very much lighter cord than formerly. Whereas at one time greased clothes-line or sash-cord was widely employed for this purpose, my suggestion is that nylon cord is a much better bet, being stronger and lighter, less liable to kinks and with a far longer life. Indeed, a nylon cord not much thicker than parcel string has almost as great a breaking strain as some of the heavy cords we used to use, and is practically rot-proof.

LEADS AND DUMMIES

The best type of training lead made is leather, good harness leather for preference, three-quarters to seven-eighths of an inch wide, about four feet long and with a metal ring or D at one end and a hand-loop at the other. The loop end is slipped through the D, forming a choke which goes round the pupil's neck and acts as a collar, tightening when the dog pulls but relaxing immediately the strain is eased. A big, strong and wilful dog may require one of the popular modern choke-chain types of collar, but for general purposes and with a dog of reasonable temperament I find my leather slips far more convenient and just as effective. Slip leads of nylon cord can also be obtained, or made by your local saddler, on the same principle as the leather lead suggested above, but though these are strong and light they are harder on the hands of the trainer (especially when teaching heel-keeping which necessitates hard jerking!) and, to me, have not the same appeal as good old leather. One useful tip about leather leads: keep them dressed with neatsfoot or Mars oil and they will remain supple and last for years.

Early retrieving work – and even advanced practice – is best given to the gundog pupil by means of a dummy or 'bundle'. This accustoms the pupil to carrying an inanimate object, which offers less temptation for it to bite and play with than the real thing, is always accessible, and can be carried in the pocket and used at all seasons of the year. Small puppies must have small dummies, but size and weight can be increased as the pupil grows. The traditional training dummies, beloved by most professional handlers, are made of stuffed rabbit (or even hare) skins, or of old wool or stocking legs stuffed with rags, wood, wool or hay. Nowadays, however, a variety of dummies is used by both amateurs and professionals, and these include small canvas boat fender types, and pieces of car radiator hose. For normal training of the average well-grown spaniel or retriever the dummy should be nine to twelve inches in length and about three inches in diameter. Weights can be varied and it is not a bad idea to have various dummies weighing from eight ounces to about three or more pounds. Dummies should be softish and have a string attached for easier throwing. Artificial scenting of dummies should be avoided, for the practice makes things too easy for the pupil. A well-used dummy will quickly acquire a strong scent of its own from the trainer's hands and pocket!

The rabbit or hare skin dummy is useful to accustom a dog to retrieving fur, and I like also to make up feather dummies in order that birds may more readily be accepted when the time comes. Possibly the simplest method of doing this is to obtain a number of wings of game birds, ducks or even domestic fowls, dry them out well and attach them by means of strong rubber bands or string to a length of car radiator hosepipe, or to rolled-up sacking. The reader can give full play to his ingenuity in making up dummies, remembering that for water work he must use something that will float, and during advanced practice the ordinary tennis ball can prove very useful as a training medium. Not only can it be conveniently carried in the pocket, available for use at odd moments, but it can be thrown long distances and, since it will roll and bounce, it can be made to offer more difficult and interesting retrieves than the standard article.

THE GUN

Of course, a gundog in training has to be accustomed to the sound of gunfire and, later, to dropping to shot if used for questing. It is also important that the pupil should become used to the handler carrying and flourishing the weapon. Nowadays we are fortunate in being able to obtain special blank cartridges (which are very much cheaper and safer than live ammunition) for use in the standard shotgun. These blanks are of .22 calibre, obtainable with varying charges, and together with adapter to fit the shotgun chamber can be supplied by the manufacturers, Messrs Turner-Richards, Cardigan Street, Birmingham 4.

Besides the Turner-Richards shotgun adapter and training blanks, this enterprising company also markets very useful blank-firing pistols, an essential item of equipment for any serious gundog trainer who fires a considerable number of blanks and likes to be able to accustom his pupils to doubles or even a succession of quick shots, thus simulating conditions likely to be met on a day's shooting. The advantage that the T-R blanks offer over the starter's pistol type is that they produce a realistic bang rather than a rifle crack, of which many puppies show an immediate and intense dislike. They also enable the trainer to use his ordinary shotgun in the dual role, and save both money and trouble. The subjects of gunfire and teaching dropping to shot are dealt with in Chapter 3.

THE DUMMY-LAUNCHER

Many enthusiastic trainers – both amateur and professional – nowadays make use of the dummy-launcher for teaching marking and long retrieves, and accustoming their pupils to the sound of gunfire. This apparatus resembles the 'beer-can' launcher, a special dummy being fitted over a spigot and ejected by the blast of a .22 blank cartridge. Obtainable from most gunmakers and sporting goods shops, the launcher is a versatile piece of equipment which can be put to many uses, and is a good investment for anyone who wishes to train his dog to a high degree of efficiency. The model I use and recommend is manufactured by Messrs Turner-Richards of Birmingham.

WORDS OF COMMAND

Decide upon your words of command and whistles before you attempt to train your puppy. Choose suitable ones and stick to them. Commands are best kept short, sharp and simple. 'Sit', 'heel', 'no', 'fetch', 'get in', 'get over', 'get out', 'go back' and 'kennel' are the ones I use and find satisfactory, and they are self-explanatory.

Whistles can be used in many different ways and are discussed in a later chapter. Suffice it to suggest here that for simplicity and convenience you use an artificial whistle: one blast to make the dog sit, a series of short toots to recall it, and a couple of quick toots to attract its attention when it is out questing.

2

Early Obedience Work

OBEDIENCE LESSONS

Having obtained your puppy, got him home and made him comfortable, give him two or three weeks to get used to his new surroundings before starting the training course. If you have only one dog and want to get the best out of him, have him about with you and let him live indoors. There is a widely held belief that a gundog should live in a kennel until fully trained, but experience has taught me that this is a fallacy and, providing that he is treated sensibly and not allowed liberties or to be petted by strangers, you will get far more out of him by treating him as a stable companion, and he will get into your ways much more quickly.

After the usual house training, which is quickly learned if the pup is let out every two or three hours for a short spell and scolded every time he offends, the early obedience lessons may commence. I find it useful to accustom him to his bed by constantly putting him in it, saying 'bed', 'kennel' or what you will, and holding him down for several minutes, pointing to the bed and putting him back every time he clambers out. Soon he will bed down to command. All sorts of little obedience lessons can be taught like this indoors. When a command has been given, show the pup what is meant, and after he has grasped the idea see that he obeys every time. Do not use a loud tone of voice and never beat him. A slap does no harm to a stolid dog but a thrashing may easily ruin him.

During the early walks, keep the pup on a lead and make him walk in the desired position at heel, on your left side. If he runs or lags behind jerk the lead, haul him back and command 'Heel'.

After a few lessons he will follow naturally and you can then let the lead trail, stepping on it when he runs ahead. This gives him a jerk, and he will soon learn to heel. Here a distinction between a retriever and a spaniel is noticeable. My experience has taught me that a retriever learns to heel easily and will thereafter stick close to you, but a spaniel likes to wander off at an angle or lag behind unless constantly checked. If you have a spaniel pup, therefore, you must be vigilant and keep up the training longer, and check any disobedience at the outset. I suppose so many generations of retrievers have been at heel so long that it is now instinctive with them! Signs are always useful, and so when commanding heel swing your left arm and point to heel. Soon the sign alone will suffice to bring your pupil in.

'Sit' is the next item on the programme. Take the pup on the lawn or into a field, and push him down on his haunches, holding him there awhile, at the same time raising your right hand and commanding, 'sit' (or any suitable word you like providing you stick to the same one). Gradually he will learn to go down on command, and you can then try edging away from him, returning and putting him back in position each time he gets up to follow you. This must be done every time without exception. The pup must learn that you mean what you say and that to hear is to obey. These lessons should not last longer than ten or fifteen minutes, but can be repeated two or three times a day, and even indoors on wet days and at odd moments. With a very obstinate puppy it is sometimes necessary to peg down – that is, tie him by a short lead so that when he rises to follow you he cannot do so – but I find the lesson better learned without this if possible. Always give the signal with the command. Later, when the dog knows he is doing wrong in leaving his drop, I haul him back rather roughly by the collar, so that he is dancing on his hind legs. This has a psychological effect which seldom fails, and is much more effective than slaps and beatings. I am a great believer in tone of voice adjustment to suit the occasion. Speak gruffly and grumblingly when your pupil is at fault, and pleasantly when he is doing well. A loud voice is most undesirable, and the pup will soon learn by your tone if he is in favour or not.

The aim is to teach your pupil to drop sharply to voice, whistle or signal wherever he may be, and to stay in that position until it suits you to move him, even when out of sight. Only by constant practice and patience can this be achieved, and gradually the pup will drop to command when running ahead of you at exercise, and let you get out of sight. It is as well to keep this lesson up even during his first shooting season, and whenever he is with you a few drops will do good. Through lack of space I have rather condensed this exercise and made it appear easy. It is easy, but it is a long job, and until a pup will drop to command or signal no other lesson should be taught except heeling and dummy work.

An excitable young pup that will sit to command during his lessons, but when running ahead takes no notice of the command, should have a twenty-five-yard check cord attached, and be checked with the command. A check cord is useful for the early lessons to prevent the pup rushing off, and sometimes later for field work. This depends largely on the pup himself – I find that ninety per cent do not require it. However, your will must be enforced at all times, and the check cord is the best method, *if not overdone*. Remember to check any bad habit immediately, and to reseat the pup in exactly the same position as before when he leaves his drop without orders. I am not a believer in giving tit-bits as a reward for good work if it can be avoided. I find the pup thinks more about the treat to come than the work in hand, but in some cases it is helpful to encourage a dull pup this way.

Teaching the gundog puppy to sit to command and signal requires, as I have said, a good deal of time and patience, but as it is one of the most essential accomplishments, the trainer will do well to keep up the exercise until it has been completely mastered. Of course puppies vary tremendously in their aptitude, and some dogs hate sitting still while others quickly take to dropping to command.

Constant repetition and patience will eventually wear the pupil's resistance until one can imagine him saying to himself, 'I might just as well sit tight until ordered on, or I shall only be hauled back again and be longer than ever getting away to play.' It is no good only dragging him back to his original position occasionally – it must be done every time the puppy gets up without orders.

Most puppies, if taught to sit thoroughly while the trainer is close at hand, will go down to command when at a distance and running free. However, it is just as well to teach him what is required, even though it is perhaps the most boring lesson for both trainer and trainee. Have your puppy on the usual training ground, and make him sit. Walk away twenty yards, turn round and call him up. When he is nearly up to you, give the signal and sharp command to sit. Repeat this, each time getting a little farther away from him and giving the command earlier and earlier until he will go down when halfway to you. Ultimately you will be able to seat him at quite a considerable distance by command and signal and later by signal alone.

It is at times most helpful to have a guiding star, in the person of a fully trained dog whom your pupil can watch going through his paces, dropping to command, staying at the drop for an indefinite period, and so on. This asset will probably not be readily obtainable to the majority of trainers who are teaching a dog for their own use, but I mention it in case a shining example could be obtained to demonstrate what is required to a slow puppy. These apparently dull specimens which one occasionally comes across are not really lacking in brains and usually become excellent workers once they understand what is required, but they are a long time grasping the idea. I have found that for weeks they appear stupid, when suddenly something seems to snap in their brain and they cotton on wonderfully. Do not despair, then, if your pupil is a little dopey at first. Keep your wool on, and persevere.

I have previously mentioned the advantages of having your pupil with you as much as possible, in order that he may grow to love and respect you, and you for your part can watch his development and learn his ways. When out with the puppy for a walk, see that he sits steadily while you chat to any friend that you meet, and discourage him from going up to every dog. You can teach him patience at the drop by seating him outside a door whenever you call at a friend's house, or the local, always providing that you peer out at him now and again and do not leave him in peril from traffic. It is most useful to have a dog that can be taken anywhere, and he should be accustomed to buses, trains and cars at an early age. I do not consider it fair on the dog, however well trained you may have made him, to take him among traffic without a lead, and the owner who takes unnecessary risks is a fool to himself.

I should like to stress the importance of having the puppy under training free from worms and skin parasites. No dog will give his best if not one hundred per cent fit; worms cause all sorts of complications and make the dog easily tired and listless, and skin parasites take his mind of his work – nothing is more exasperating than having to await the fulfilment of a command while the pupil scratches his ear or bites his hocks. Even though there may be no signs of worms, I advise the periodical administration of a vermifuge, and regular dusting of both the dog and his bed with one of the powdered disinfectants recommended for this purpose. Regular grooming is advisable, too, and any suspicious spot or sore should be treated immediately. During the summer watch for sore feet, and after every outing run your hands over his coat for thorns. All these precautions may appear elementary, but it is surprising how often they are neglected even by experienced dog owners.

To return to actual lessons, we are now at the stage where our pupil has been taught to heel, sit to command and sit at a distance, and we are practising him for steadiness on the drop while we are out of sight at odd times. Presently I will deal with the use of the whistle and hand signals, as well as general obedience. Dummy work merits a section to itself, and is in any case best postponed until the puppy has fairly mastered the lessons already outlined. There is a reason for the order in which I am giving the various exercises, as each one is intended to draw out the pupil's brainpower and memory a little, step by step, but I must harrow old ground again and ask you not to try and teach too much at once or his mind will become muddled. Short but frequent spells of education are more beneficial to dogs as well as children, especially if the subjects are varied and made as interesting as possible.

It would be as well to warn you that if perchance your puppy is in the habit of picking up and carrying about gloves or other similar articles left lying about, he should never be chased and have the object grabbed roughly from his mouth, and on no account should he be beaten after picking up and carrying anything. If you do this, you are in danger of spoiling him for retrieving, which must at all costs be avoided. Your common sense should tell you how best to deal with any such situation as may arise, but you cannot be too careful.

Before proceeding with the next item on the training programme – dummy work – I think that a few general hints and instructions will not come amiss. I hope I shall be forgiven if throughout these pages I stress the psychological aspect of dog training but, after all, this is the most important point and the one most generally overlooked. The trainer who gets inside his dog's mind is the man who will produce the best results, and in doing so he will obtain added interest and valuable lessons in self-discipline.

It is generally accepted that dogs vary in character just as much as human beings, with the exception that there are fewer bad characters in the canine species. With the working breeds, personality is more pronounced, because generations have been taught and encouraged to use their thinking boxes. It is impossible to train any dog by set rules for this reason; although the rudiments of the course can be laid down, the application will have to vary to suit individual dogs. This is why it is so extremely important that throughout the training course you constantly note your puppy's reaction to your methods. The gundog is a delicate piece of mechanism; whereas with a car you can get it put right at the garage if a fault develops, no such easy way out is possible with a dog!

Perhaps a simple illustration will give the reader some idea of what I am getting at. I had a spaniel brought to me by a worried owner, who told me that his dog (about one year old) was a splendid retriever and very obedient, but that nothing would induce him to face thick prickly cover, and he was therefore useless. During conversation it came out that when a pup of six months or so this dog was timid and, having failed to get him into thick cover by methods of persuasion, the irate handler lost his temper and pitched the pup bodily into the middle of a clump of brambles. I ask you! Needless to say, I gave the owner a piece of my mind, and refused the task of trying to cure a fault which need never have been implanted had the owner waited until the pup was keen enough on his work to enter cover of his own accord, or borrowed a courageous dog to use as an example. And this sort of unthinking foolishness to a good dog is perpetrated every day by quite humane, but impatient, dog trainers. The whole essence of training is to promote a love of work in the dog, and nothing that might in any way impair a puppy's keenness should ever be done – and small things count more than is generally realized.

It should be obvious that during these early lessons in obedience the rate of progress should be adjusted to suit the response of the pupil, and it is hopeless to start retrieving lessons until the puppy will come instantly when called by name or whistled. So, during these early days, every effort must be made to attain this object. Some dogs are responsive to call from the first and give little trouble. Others are inclined to be independent and must be made to see that, when they are called, instant obedience is expected. To do this, a light check cord some twenty-five yards long should be used. When at exercise ahead of you, the pup is called by name, or whistled softly, or both alternately. The end of the cord is stood on, and the puppy hauled in, when a great fuss must be made of him. Keep him at heel for a few minutes and repeat the lesson. Try to dispense with the cord as soon as possible, because there is always the danger of the pup realizing that he is only under command when it is on. When the sitting lesson is well learned, there is another and better method of obtaining instant response, but this will be dealt with later.

Hand signals are invaluable, and here again you can devise your own so long as you ensure that they are unmistakable to the dog and that the same one is always used for the same command. Like the whistle, too much cannot be expected at first, but by beginning as you intend to go on you are training the dog unconsciously, and he must not be muddled by indistinct or varying orders and signals.

By alternating the various lessons and utilizing odd moments to practise the pup in those already learned, you are going a long way towards preventing his becoming bored and mechanical in his response. It is not desirable to turn your pup into a robot, whose actions are unthinkingly automatic; you should let him retain his initiative and merely adapt his natural ability to suit your own ends. Once again, let me say that the lessons should be short but frequent, and that it is preferable to do everything for your pup personally. Nobody but the trainer should ever exercise him if it can possibly be avoided, and certainly do not allow others to interfere with his training. You have got to be boss now and always, and be looked to for pleasure and guidance; see to it that your puppy is not spoiled by the good intentions of others.

It is not a bad idea to train a gundog to drop to a sharp blast on the whistle. This can prove very useful when working the dog in dense cover, and is, of course, less disturbing to game than the voice. Apart from this, dropping to whistle is a very showy accomplishment and the hallmark of the well-trained dog. If one is going to do this, I suggest that you use a pea-whistle, which can be slung round the neck on a cord, or attached to the button-hole and kept in the breast pocket. If a whistle is used for dropping the dog, you will obviously have to use either a different whistle or, better still, a mouth-made whistle, for attracting his attention and calling him to heel. I suggest, therefore, that the pea-whistle is kept solely for dropping the dog, and that a short natural chirp be used to attract the dog's attention when hunting, and a longer natural whistle to bring him to heel. I have found that this works very well.

However, many of our handlers who, like myself, are in the unfortunate position of being unable to produce effective mouth whistles (owing to advancing years and loss of natural teeth!) can and do achieve remarkably effective results by using but one whistle for dropping, turning (whilst questing) and recalling their dogs. To this end, the single sharp blast is used for dropping; two quick toots for turning and a series of short, sharp and urgent blasts for recalling . . . all on the same whistle. There are several types of artificial whistle from which to choose, and selection of one is a matter for individual preference. You can obtain anything from the very high-pitched, practically inaudible silent type through plastic referee-type whistles to the metal scout or police pattern. These days I myself use practically nothing but the plastic, small Acme 'Thunderer' pea-whistle or its American counterpart, and it is truly surprising what variation in volume and note can be achieved on the same whistle after a little practice.

To teach a dog to drop to whistle is comparatively simple. Once dropping is taught in the ordinary way the whistle can be introduced, and blown sharply either just before or just after the command to drop, and in conjunction with the raised hand signal. In a very short while the dog will learn to respond to the whistle alone; indeed, I have found that many dogs respond far more quickly to an order conveyed via the whistle than to one conveyed by voice.

A QUESTION OF MOUTH

The all-important question of mouth, hard or soft, causes the gundog trainer many anxious moments and, while a dog that badly mangles his game is useless as a retriever, the dog that merely gives his game a good grip can be used. However, it is much more enjoyable to own a really tender-mouthed dog, and it should not be difficult to do so.

Experience goes to show that the great majority of dogs are naturally tender-mouthed, but congenital hard-mouthed specimens are found, and here parentage plays an important part; given a puppy of good working parents, it is more often than not the trainer's fault if he turns out hard-mouthed, and this is more so in the case of spaniels than retrievers.

What can the trainer do, then, to try and ensure that his young pupil will do him credit and retrieve tenderly? Perhaps the cardinal rule is always to be as gentle as possible in your actions with the puppy, and to take his dummy, or anything else that he is carrying, as though you were handling precious eggs! Never, never snatch anything from his mouth, even though he be running round with your wife's only pair of unladdered stockings! Command him to bring it to you and receive it graciously. I make a point, when giving my young dogs their breakfast of hard biscuit, to make them sit, take the biscuit gently from me, and await the command to scamper away and eat it. This simple lesson has a twofold object – to teach the puppies to take things up gently, and to impress upon them that I am boss and that they must await my pleasure before enjoying their meal. Incidentally, they have to sit and look at their suppers until the word of command, too. The puppy that snatches his biscuit from my hand receives a flip on the nose and the command, 'gently', and the biscuit is withdrawn until the request is complied with. It is surprising how quickly they come to understand what is required.

The dog that lives indoors frequently gets hold of a glove or scarf that someone has dropped, and walks round with it in his mouth. The owner of the article in question usually makes a dive at the puppy and grabs it away. The pup naturally resents anyone but master taking anything from him (and indeed he should be made to realize that master is the one to whom all retrieves should be delivered) and grips harder than ever. Make a point of taking everything from your dog personally, and make your family realize that during your absence he should be treated with common sense. The puppy must at all times be encouraged to retrieve, and never beaten for doing so even, as I have said, if he is carrying round some precious article.

While on the subject of hard and soft mouths, and although this advice on training is still only in the hand-work stage, I should like to add a few remarks about the retrieving of game and its effect upon the dog's mouth. Never under any circumstances send an inexperienced dog for a wounded and jumping bird or rabbit – make sure that it is stone dead before he goes out. If on the first occasion of retrieving flesh and blood the dog stops and mouths the game or starts tearing it to pieces, do not rush up and grab at the game. Run away in the opposite direction, calling him to follow.

I hold very strong views on the mouth question, and I am certain that many puppies put down as hard-mouthed are not really so but that they treat their game roughly from sheer excitement. I have trained many dogs that bit and tore their first few birds, but with experience settled down and became perfect retrievers. Excitable dogs should have less retrieving than stolid dogs, and it is advisable to keep up the hand training longer than would normally be the case. Far more dogs are spoiled by too much retrieving than by too little. A dog that gives up his game willingly is usually tender-mouthed, and quite often they will retrieve stone-dead and cold game tenderly but bite any fresh or kicking. Experience will probably put all this right. Whatever others may say I most severely condemn thrashing an inexperienced dog for biting game; the object of your lessons is to instil a love of retrieving, but after a beating a dog will always feel nervous when bringing in his game.

Do not under any consideration force open a pup's mouth and shove in an object that he refuses to lift. If persuasion will not do the trick, force surely will not. Give him time, and if possible let him see a good retriever at work. If he refuses to give up the game make him sit and stroke his head, talking softly all the time. Try everything before putting a finger and thumb on each side of his jaw and gently pressing his lips against his teeth to make him relax his hold. The trainer must always consider the effect his actions will have on the puppy.

PSYCHOLOGICAL PUNISHMENT

The understanding gundog handler very quickly gets into the habit of studying his pupil's temperament, and by the time a puppy is seven or eight months old he notices all kinds of odd little characteristics about his dog. Annoying habits often begin to form at this age, and the question of suitable punishment has to be seriously considered.

There are some who hold that punishment has no place in the training of a puppy, while others, I regret to say, regard the whip as their most useful training implement. I agree with neither school of thought, but prefer the middle course which suggests that punishment is at times most necessary, always providing that the culprit thoroughly understands the reason for its administration, and that the chastisement is carried out in the right place geographically. Just punishment at the right place and time will increase your authority over your dog, who will respect you and bear no ill-will, whereas unconsidered beatings will have just the opposite effect.

During the early months of training the puppy should be guided in the way he should go and the slightest show of physical force will more than likely cow him. Firmness is usually all that is necessary during this time, but the trainer should make quite sure that his pupil thoroughly understands his commands; otherwise his mistakes will be taken for wilfulness, with unfortunate results. It is impossible to expect a young dog to understand a command unless he has previously been shown clearly what is meant; do not credit your puppy with more brains than he has got.

By the time he comes on to field work, a puppy is old enough to stand just punishment without becoming cowed, but a slight mistake will have unhappy results. To illustrate what I mean, I will instance a very foolish action on my part some time ago, which gave a puppy the wrong idea and caused me a lot of unnecessary work to undo the harm I had unwittingly committed. I was out with two pupils, one a mature Labrador sent to me to cure unsteadiness to shot, the other a puppy just at the stage of learning to drop to shot. In my ignorance I thought it a good opportunity to test both dogs, and so when both were running ahead of me I fired a shot. The puppy dropped like a stone, but the Labrador who should have known better went charging out blindly. I adopted my usual practice and awaited his return, and then took him by the throat and dragged him rather roughly to the spot where he was when he ran in, and proceeded to give him a few strokes with a leather lead, grumbling and grousing at him. While doing this I was amazed to find the puppy crawling towards us on his stomach, and when he got up to me he lay on his back with his legs in the air, obviously terrified. After that, he refused to leave my side for the rest of the lesson, keeping his tail between his legs and showing signs of serious nervousness. Later, I fired again; the Labrador, having profited by his correction, remained steady, but the puppy took to his heels and bolted for home.

The moral is obvious. By my display of violence to the older dog, who well understood what the correction was for, I had implanted in the mind of the puppy a connection between a gunshot and a whipping, and I can tell you that I had a month's hard work to eradicate this wrong impression from his immature mind. It was not gunshyness or nervousness – just the belief that when I fired it was a signal for a beating; there was, of course, nothing to tell the puppy that the older dog was in the wrong. I learned a lot from this incident, and I now make a point of never punishing a dog in view of another unless *both* are aware of the reason for it.

The best method of correcting a dog is actually to catch him in the act of doing wrong and chastise immediately, but this is often impossible. The next best thing is to take him to the actual spot of his indiscretion and punish him there, grumbling at him meanwhile, giving a long period of sitting afterwards for meditation. By taking him to the scene of the crime you are impressing upon his mind the reason for the punishment, and it will make a lasting impression. Never, under any circumstances, hit your dog when he returns to you, or you will find that soon he will keep out of reach and even drop game that he is retrieving rather than come to hand. Let him come up to you, take him by the collar or put on a lead, and drag him roughly to the spot where he erred. If this paragraph be cut out and hung in a large frame over the door of every trainer's kennels we should, I am sure, see fewer spoiled dogs and harassed trainers; even some of the old hands are guilty of unconscious idiocy when it comes to the question of punishment.

The check cord is very useful for catching a dog in the act of crime, and by the intelligent use of it he can often be punished at the right moment. I need hardly add that it is better to give no punishment at all than to do so some time after the offence, and that the less punishment the excitable dog has the better. The trainer who relies upon the whip to obtain obedience from his pupils stands out as an obvious and admitted failure. Few of us would send our sons to a school where we knew the cane would be used indiscriminately and without good reason; why then subject our dog, who has far less reasoning power than a child, to unnecessary harshness in the attempt to get obedience?

I have used a lot of space in the discussion of punishment, but in reality I have not said half enough, as it is over this matter that the majority of dogs are ruined by their handlers. I ask every owner, handler and trainer of gundogs to punish only when essential, at the right time and in the correct place, and never do so in anger. If this is carried out your dogs will do you credit anywhere, and you will for evermore be loved, honoured and obeyed. What, I ask, could be sweeter reward to the student of canine psychology?

3

Retrieving

TRAINING THE YOUNG DOG

The subject of retrieving is one which is very dear to the gundog man, and nothing catches the eye of the spectators at a shoot more than a dog galloping out, picking up and returning to hand at speed. All the same, in my opinion too much emphasis is often laid upon the retrieving side of a gundog's work, to the detriment of other more or equally important considerations.

Take the case of the roughshooter's spaniel (retriever, or other breed used to hunt-up game). Surely the first essential here is game-finding ability, because unless game is flushed none will be shot, and there will be nothing to retrieve anyway! But I have met with roughshooters who were far more concerned about their dog's retrieving than about his game-finding. Steadiness, too, is sometimes disregarded providing the dog retrieves, but an unsteady dog which chases every head of game will spoil a great number of shots, and the fact that he may be a perfect retriever does not atone for the loss of game. For every head of game a dog is called upon to retrieve (or should be called upon to retrieve, but more of this anon), there will be four or five head flushed.

Some people (one might almost say a good many) send their dogs to retrieve quite unnecessarily. I have seen dogs sent for a bird lying in the open not twenty yards from the gun, which anyone could have picked up. To send a dog to retrieve stuff which he has seen fall and lies where he can rely on sight alone is one of the surest ways of teaching him to run in to shot, and to discourage him from persevering when he cannot plainly see the object of his retrieve. Is it a love of showmanship, laziness or just pure ignorance that so many people allow (nay, encourage!) their dogs to retrieve unnecessarily?

Useless retrieving, besides the disadvantages mentioned above, will frequently bore a young dog, and he becomes slow. Familiarity can breed contempt, and that is why the less retrieving the young dog is given (once it is assured that he can and will retrieve) the better. Even so, the retrieves he is called upon to carry out must be chosen with care and, though easy ones at first are the rule, one should gradually work up to sending the dog only for something which is well hidden (if not completely lost), and which will require the fullest use of nose to find. If we continually give a dog easy retrieves, then he will soon give up when he does not quickly come upon the stuff, and after all the object of a gundog is to find game which is either inaccessible to the shooter or completely lost. I do not think it can be too seriously or too often stressed that useless retrieving is an abomination and bad for the dog in every respect.

I have mentioned before the folly of putting a dog on to a runner which is still in sight. It not only encourages chase but makes the dog reliant upon his eyes instead of his nose, though any dog worth his salt will start using his nose directly his eyes fail him. But a young dog is very impressionable, and once put on to a runner which is still in view he will ever after be inclined to run in or chase and to use his eyes before his nose. I was recently asked if a dog could not be allowed to gather a dead rabbit lying out beyond the buries while ferreting – but with what object? If the rabbit is dead, then it can wait until ferreting is finished and be gathered by hand. If it is alive, then give it another barrel rather than risking unsteadying the dog by allowing him to retrieve a runner by sight. It is a mistake to think that because a dog will retrieve he has got to be used every time something is down, and one which has led to the ruination of many a good dog.

Dummy work in the early stages can very easily be overdone, and a great many puppies are called upon to retrieve a thrown dummy again and again, until they tire. Little wonder that they become slow retrievers, or worse still occasional retrievers who sometimes will and sometimes will not pick up! Once a puppy will gallop out and pick up the dummy and return with it to hand, then it should seldom be asked to retrieve from the open. Hide the dummy in cover, drop it and send him back for it, throw it over a hedge into cover – ring the changes as often as possible, but do not keep letting him retrieve the dummy from open ground.

Even so, do not overdo these lessons. Once a day for a few minutes is better than twice a week for half an hour. Encourage a speedy return, either by running away and whistling or calling the pup, or by hiding yourself – a dog retrieves quicker when he finds himself lost.

Delivery is an important part of retrieving, not because of appearances so much as because it is annoying to have a dog which either stands just out of reach and perhaps drops the game, or one which makes rings round his master and hangs on to the game like grim death. The first fault is usually the result of fear – the dog has been hurt at some time when delivering to hand, or his master is too wedded to the whip, and he does not like to come within striking distance. The second fault is more common, and is in part due to a reluctance to give up the delightful object he is carrying and partly to show off. Notice how proudly the circling retriever struts with his game! This can be overcome by walking on and taking the retrieve from the dog whilst on the move, or by giving him lessons in a dead end where there is no room to circle. With a shy dog it may be due to the presence of strangers near his master.

I like the idea of a dog coming well up to hand and sitting to deliver. With a confident puppy this can quite easily be taught by getting him well up to hand, putting a hand under his chin and ordering him to drop. Many dogs will sit and hold their game quite tenderly at their master's feet until he is ready to take it.

However necessary it is to make a dog into a good and finished retriever, it should not be taught retrieving to the exclusion of some of the other necessary qualifications. Game must be found – if it can be found and retrieved smartly, so much the better.

Retrieving practice with the dummy has been dealt with by many authorities in the past, and gallons of ink have been lavished on the extreme caution needed throughout this exercise. Despite this, there are still many wrong conceptions, and I can safely bet that more dogs have been spoiled by too much dummy practice than by too little.

It should, perhaps, be explained that the use of a dummy for the early retrieving lessons is necessary, because some medium less exciting than flesh and blood must be used, and the stuffed stocking is easily portable and light enough for a small puppy to lift. Straw, wood wool, or some similar material should be used to stuff the stocking, which must be sewn up at the end. A stuffed rabbit skin may be used if desired, as explained earlier.

Retrieving lessons can be given once the puppy has fairly mastered the simple obedience exercises already outlined, but these latter must not be neglected while dummy work is in progress. It is as well to mix the different lessons as much as possible, to prevent boredom on the part of the pupil (and teacher) and to cultivate his memory.

Like all early lessons, retrieving practice is best carried out on the lawn or in a field where there is nothing to distract the puppy's attention, and should be short but progressive. A light check cord *can* be used during the early stages, *but should be discontinued as soon as the puppy shows no inclination to run in to the fall of the dummy.* Although the check cord is a most useful item of the dog trainer's equipment, it should not be used more than necessary, or the dog will become conscious of it and consequently cunning when worked free.

We now have our puppy on the lawn (perhaps wearing his check cord) and, we hope, in a pleasant and receptive frame of mind. One or two drops and a walk round at heel will suffice to remind him that discipline is being maintained, and he can then be seated close in front of the trainer, who holds the ends of the check cord under one foot in case of accidents. The dummy is taken from its hiding-place and the puppy allowed to sniff at it, after which it should be thrown a few yards, to fall on open ground. Any attempt to race after it on the part of the puppy is restrained by the check cord, and he is reseated. About thirty seconds is allowed to elapse, and then a wave of the hand and the previously decided word of command sends him out. In all probability he will pick up the dummy and return in triumph with his prize. If so, well and good. Take it from him very gently, speaking coaxingly all the time, and make a great fuss of him when he has released his hold.

It is possible that this happy result is not accomplished, but instead he walks round you in circles and will not come to hand. Caution! Do not make the all-too-common fatal mistake of rushing after him and snatching the dummy away. Instead run off in the opposite direction, calling to the pup to follow. In most cases he will do so, and will allow you to take the dummy. If he does not respond to this dodge, you must tempt him with a piece of biscuit, but try your utmost to do without bribery, as it often results in the dropping of the dummy at some distance in excitement to get at the biscuit. In any case, cease feeding the dog the moment he understands what is required. Another possibility is that your pupil may not lift the dummy, but will lie down and start tearing it and playing with it. The same remedy can be applied and is nearly always successful. A puppy of good working stock is seldom troublesome during his lesson, but even these dogs sometimes refuse to deliver the dummy willingly and hold on for dear life. If he is then commanded to sit, caressed, and coaxed, the dummy can be gradually slid from his mouth. Never, never pull and tug anything from his mouth, or you will surely ruin him as a retriever.

There remains the case of the exceptional puppy who refuses to lift the dummy at all. Above all things, do not force him – be patient and hope that he will come to it, as he almost certainly will, especially if you can borrow a keen retrieving dog to hold up as a shining example. Allow him to run in to the thrown dummy if he desires to do so.

No opportunity should ever be lost for impressing upon a puppy under training that you set the time and give the orders, and making him wait before retrieving is just one method of doing this, besides cultivating the habit of steadiness. Two or three successful retrieves per lesson are quite sufficient and, once the puppy behaves himself and delivers willingly, cease throwing the dummy in full sight of him. Let him be made to seek for it hidden in long grass or other cover, ensuring at first that the wind is in his favour. Later still the dummy can be dropped in full sight of the puppy when he is out for a walk at heel. Walk him on for about twenty yards before you send him back for it, and gradually increase the distance and the interval until he will go back two hundred yards after ten minutes' wait. When you get to this stage you are well on the road to success.

Willing delivery can be encouraged by calling up whenever you spot the puppy at play carrying an object in his mouth, which should be taken gently, and returned to him for further play after a pat and an encouraging word. The dummy lessons must on no account be overdone, or he will become sloppy and careless in his retrieving, and once he is proficient in the above exercises an occasional retrieve is all that is necessary. Do not try and show off in front of your friends by making him retrieve again and again (which is very often done), and if you do, you deserve the usual result, which is that the dog refuses to do anything right!

GUNFIRE AND DROPPING TO SHOT

In the training of a gundog puppy, one of the things most frequently ignored or hurried over is dropping to shot. Most shooting men will, I think, agree that dropping to shot is an important item in the training course – essential for a questing dog and even desirable in a retriever.

So often the puppy is started off all wrong – by this, I mean that the report of the gun becomes a signal for a retrieve instead of, as it should be, an order to drop. If, therefore, a puppy is trained from a very early age that a bang means he must drop sharply, one of the most annoying habits of the mature gundog – running in to shot – can be avoided, or at any rate labelled as a definite offence so that any correction administered is understood and taken to heart.

It is quite a good idea to get a puppy accustomed to firing as a signal for his meals, or during his mealtime, when his attention is focused upon something pleasant. If one teaches the puppy to sit and await orders before eating his supper, as I do, the shot can be introduced as a supplementary piece of training, and then we have three things connected in the dog's mind – a shot, a drop and something pleasant – in other words, his food. In a large kennel this may not be practicable, but I do most strongly recommend this method to the owner of a single puppy.

In my own case, puppies become accustomed to firing almost from the nest stage, as my rabbit pen and training ground are not far from the kennels, and consequently they grow up inured to the sound of gunfire. The average man will have to proceed a little more cautiously.

In the first instance of introduction to gunfire, I suggest that the owner stays with the pup, fondling him and giving him a piece of biscuit, whilst a friend walks away fifty yards or so and fires. If the puppy shows no fear the distance can be decreased, but it there is any display of nerves the procedure will have to be repeated at increased distances and the puppy made confident by stroking and appeal to the inner dog.

Once the puppy can stand gunfire at close quarters, he should either be taught at mealtimes to drop to shot, as suggested above, or be pushed down every time the pistol or gun is fired. If he has already been taught to drop to command then everything is very much easier, for all one has to do is to fire and at the same time give the verbal command to drop. The raised hand signal is useful, too, because the gun or pistol can be raised and so give a definite drop signal.

It is surprising how quickly a puppy learns to go down to shot, and equally surprising how slack he will become about this once field work is commenced. Dropping to shot must be insisted upon all through the training course, and possibly for some time thereafter.

Once the puppy will drop to shot when his master is close by, he should be left on the drop while the trainer walks away twenty or thirty paces, and then called up. When he is halfway to the trainer the pistol can be thrown up and fired, the verbal command being given at the same time if an immediate response to the shot is not made. Daily practice makes perfect, but it is not advisable to overdo the dropping to shot lessons while the dog is in the early stages of field work, or he may become slow through always expecting the gun to be fired. This I only discovered through hard experience with several cases!

Unless a dog will drop smartly when no game is present, it is hardly likely that he will learn to do so under more exciting conditions in the field. I often tell owners of dogs sent for training that a dog efficiently taught to drop to shot can always be stopped, even at the expense of a wasted cartridge, when he starts to chase or run in. For, properly learned, the report of the pistol or gun is more effective than the spoken word or whistle as a means of securing a prompt drop. The whole idea is to let a shot convey the order to drop, and not the signal to run in. Started early, and persevered with, this lesson is certainly the most valuable to both dog and trainer. During these lessons there is, of course, no inducement to run in, the sound of the shot not connecting in the dog's mind as yet with retrieving or game. This connection will have to come ultimately when he starts work, and it is therefore imperative that he is deceived until the latest possible moment. Once a dog has tasted the delights of chase, it is very difficult to obtain steadiness without resorting to harsh methods which will cause a certain amount of misunderstanding in the dog's mind.

There is a lesson that can be given which I will leave to the discretion of the trainer, as I have never been able to decide if it is really necessary and have found no appreciable difference in ability between dogs that have and have not been brought up to it. This lesson requires the assistance of someone concealed behind a hedge to throw dummies up in the air, which the trainer fires at whilst the dog is, in the first instance, sitting by his side, and later running ahead. A quick drop must be achieved, and the puppy may be allowed to retrieve the dummy once or twice, but certainly not after every shot, and the usual interval of waiting must be observed. The advantage of this exercise is that it teaches marking but, after all, what gundog worthy of the name does not mark naturally as soon as he starts work proper? The disadvantage from my point of view is that the connection between a shot and something to retrieve is speeded up, that the work has to be carried out probably some distance from home, and that a willing assistant is not always forthcoming. A specially constructed spring thrower, fired by a string pulled by the trainer, dispenses with the necessity for a human assistant, but it is doubtful if a thrower can be made to order these days, and they are certainly not things which can be bought ready-made with ease.

The non-slip retriever puppy need not be made to drop to shot, but he should receive the same early instructions to accustom him to the gun and firing, and the optional exercise if desired. One of the reasons we see so many wild dogs in the shooting field is that insufficient attention was paid to these early gun-lessons, if indeed they were given at all. I have devoted a lot of space to this subject, but I shall consider it well worth while if it will induce trainers to pay more attention to this most important item on the training curriculum. Again I must stress the necessity for patience, perseverance and common sense in this, as in all the other lessons: you will be well repaid.

INTRODUCTION TO GAME AND FOLLOWING A TRAIL

The change-over from retrieving a dummy to the real thing must be done carefully, and the best method I have found is as follows. A cold rabbit or bird, free from blood, is taken with us on a training expedition and, after a few dummy retrieves of the going-back type, the dummy is replaced by the rabbit. The pup is walked on some distance after the rabbit is dropped before he is sent back for it. If all goes well, a warm rabbit can be used next but, in the event of the puppy refusing to lift the rabbit or tearing at it, I would suggest deferring this lesson until a little later. The correct procedure for dealing with trouble of this nature will be found in the chapter devoted to field work. If, however, your puppy behaves himself, you can start giving him the very instructive scent trail lesson.

Very few amateur dog trainers realize that there is a simple way of introducing the novice puppy to the scent of game and to experience in following a line and retrieving fur and feather, which can be carried out in the garden or any field. This method saves the necessity of continual visits to a shoot, and furthermore can be carried out during the close season. I do not pretend to be the originator of this idea, but I have adapted it very successfully in numerous cases and I feel that the benefits of having your puppy efficient in this respect prior to his introduction to actual shooting will be of great benefit to many sportsmen, whose dogs get all too little practice in their art.

These days it is comparatively simple to beg a tame rabbit from a friend who breeds them, which should be freshly killed (the fresher the better, preferably still warm), and, of course, unpaunched. Having selected your training ground sometime beforehand, you proceed to lay a cord, the longer the better, but at least thirty yards long, ensuring that the far end is near some cover, a clump of grass or a bush. The rabbit is attached to the near end, and the trainer, going by a circuitous route to the far end, slowly hauls in the rabbit and deposits the carcass in the aforementioned cover. All this is, of course, carried out without your pupil being aware of it. The puppy is then fetched, and given the scent from where the drag started and encouraged with the usual command to seek or fetch. If the puppy has never before scented a rabbit it may take some little time before he gets the hang of it, and he will have to be constantly recalled from his erratic castings to the true line, but the less a puppy can be interfered with the better, and he will learn a great deal by casting about on his own. He should also have been previously allowed to sniff the rabbit and, if you have doubts that he may not retrieve it after the find, he should have had it thrown a short distance similarly to his dummy, and encouraged to bring it to hand. If, however, he has carried fur before, but not had much practice at following a line, this lesson will also prove invaluable.

One or two hints are necessary, because they may not appear obvious to the trainer. Some time should be allowed to elapse between the laying of the drag-line and the attaching of the rabbit, in order that the trainer's scent may have time to be blown away, otherwise the dog may follow the human scent instead of that of the rabbit. The trainer should remain at the starting point and not follow his puppy up, even if he is casting in the wrong direction. He should either be brought in and put on a line afresh, or directed by hand signal; otherwise, when in the shooting field, he will always be looking for help instead of relying on himself. If the pupil hesitates over the pick-up, or takes the rabbit in his mouth and starts tearing it to pieces, on no account rush up to him and take the game away. Turn on your heel and run in the opposite direction, whistling and calling the pup to follow. In most cases he will do so, in which case stop and take the rabbit from him very gently, and be sure to give him a good deal of fussing and perhaps an edible reward. Immediately you take the rabbit, however, put it out of sight or at any rate out of the pup's reach. This will prevent the annoying habit of a dog making jumps for the game after he has delivered it, a very common fault.

Finally, a word of warning. The pup does not require this practice too often, and never repeat it with the same rabbit if it can be possibly avoided. I have found that by using the same rabbit over and over again the dog comes to think that you cannot want it, and slows down in retrieving even if he does not start to bite it. The drag should be laid in a different place on each occasion, and become progressively longer.

I have found the above lesson of enormous value in the training of numerous dogs, and if properly carried out the trouble will be well repaid when you come to shoot over your dog, who will have learned to discriminate between right and wrong and whose nose will have benefited in the hard school of experience.

4

Field training

PRELIMINARY FIELD WORK

Before we go on to discuss field training it would be as well to review the training already explained and to make sure that the pupil is ready for field work. I know much of what I am going to say appears elementary, but in dog training, as in many other walks of life, it is the small things that count.

Under the intensive training system, no puppy should be put on to field work until he is up to a good standard of obedience, and here is the test I give my pupils before taking them out to hunt-up game. Of course, minor mistakes and little acts of puppyish disobedience can be ignored, or rather not ignored, but corrected later. It is quite impossible to expect any puppy with spirit (and a dull puppy will never become a brilliant worker) to knuckle under to discipline without a few attempts at resistance, and I would not give tuppence for one that did! However, to our little examination.

The dog is taken from his bed, basket, kennel or run, as the case may be, and given a brisk scamper to work off the initial high spirits. I then call him to heel, and expect him to walk with me until otherwise instructed. Should he break away he must return immediately upon command. Next, I give him a few drops, stopping dead myself each time, and expecting him to do the same. If all goes well, I next drop him and walk away about thirty yards, making a circle round him. He will probably get up occasionally in order to change his position so that he can follow my progress, but so long as he does not leave his position I am content. Should the puppy make a serious attempt to move, or follow me, he is put back to dropping lessons until completely reliable.

The third test is with the dummy, which is hidden in cover, and the puppy sent off to seek. I expect him to find it and bring it right up to hand at a gallop, releasing it willingly into my hand. If he does not do so, more dummy lessons are the programme for the next few days.

From this, I pass on to a memory test, dropping the dummy in full sight of the pupil when he is walking at heel; after a hundred yards have been covered, he is sent back for it. The last test is concerned with dropping to shot and command at a distance. This is conducted by simply sending the puppy ahead and when he is about twenty yards away commanding, 'Sit', and giving the signal at the same time. This I repeat several times, as control at a distance is more important, and making certain of his obedience at this stage will save hours of labour later on. If all goes well, I test my puppy with the gun, firing it when he is ahead and not looking in my direction. Many dogs will drop promptly, but often they simply stand still. Insist upon a complete drop if you like, but personally I am happy if my puppy stands dead still. Finally, if your pupil has had any scent-trail lessons, give him one now as a test. If he has never had one at all, I most strongly advise giving him several before starting field work.

If your puppy comes through this test with flying colours, you will be quite justified in a little self-congratulation and an extra pint or two at the local that night! Any weakness that shows up should be rectified by further hand training before thinking of starting field work.

I want to make quite clear what is meant by 'field work'. Your puppy will be expected, in due season, to quarter his ground and enter thick cover, flush game, yet remain steady thereto, drop to shot and retrieve from land and water. Many are the disappointments which will fall to your lot before this happy end is accomplished, but with perseverance, patience and common sense you should get there in the end. By field work (in the training sense) is meant the teaching, under actual shooting conditions, of these many and difficult items. Your puppy has learned what to do, how to do it, and to obey – all under conditions deprived of excitement. He has now to do all that under the most trying circumstances, and your patience is going to be strained to the limit. Steel yourself to this fact, and make a solemn promise to yourself that you will keep your temper and if you find yourself

Sitting – the most important lesson of all.

Top left: The pupil is pressed down while on the lead and the word of command uttered sharply

Top right: The handler straightens up . . .

Below: . . . and the lesson is learned after several repetitions

Remaining seated while the handler backs away a few paces in the first instance, the lead having been removed . . .

. . . and subsequently tries walking away with his back to the dog

Once the sitting exercise has been mastered, the whistle is introduced and blown immediately after the word of command, so that, ultimately, the pupil will respond to whistle alone

earning to walk to heel, on the handler's left-hand side, by tactful use of the lead

Walking lead-free, with handler watchful and ready to counter immediately there is ny attempt at disobedience

Swinging the dummy preparatory to throwing, thus gaining the pupil's attention and interest to mark

Coming right in without hesitation . . .

. . . and delivering cleanly. Note the handler's one-handed reception of the retrieve

getting angry you will put the puppy away before you do something that you may regret. I wonder how many promising pups have been spoiled in five minutes by a hasty handler on their first day in the field – thousands, no doubt. Make up your mind that, however exasperating your puppy may be, you will not fall into temptation and undo all your hard work to date.

All too many people seem to think that dog training is just teaching a puppy a few tricks at home, after which you can reach for your gun and go shooting. Nothing could be further from the truth. Careful study of the canine outlook must be made all the way along as training progresses and, if things do not turn out as you had hoped, ask yourself the reason – try to look at it in the dog's perspective; in the majority of cases you will find, as I have done, that the fault is yours – not the dog's. 'Blackmore', in one of his articles, wrote a sentence which so well conveys to the uninitiated what every dog trainer knows from bitter experience that he will, I am sure, forgive me if I reiterate it: 'More dogs become failures through well-intentioned but misapplied tactics of unsuitably minded persons than through any inherent canine weakness.' Remember this – and act accordingly.

The man who has never owned a gundog is a sore trial, as a rule, to the professional trainer, but the man who has owned one or several and is wedded to unsound ideas is even worse. A correspondent has written that his training maxim is, 'Make up your mind what you don't want your pupil to do, and see that he doesn't!' Not bad, and if only the amateur would adopt this attitude a lot of time and temper would be saved. Any weakness on the trainer's part, any relaxation of discipline in the little things during the early days, and bad habits result with surprising rapidity. You will not have to be a sergeant-major all your dog's life, but during the first year or two vigilance must be your watchword and patience your greatest virtue. When once you have grasped these fundamental principles you are as nearly ready as your dog to start on field work.

I have endeavoured to put my human pupils in the right frame of mind for field work, and many there are who will, in due course, write and tell me that I made it sound much too hard and far too complicated! Be that as it may, I would far rather overemphasize the difficulties likely to be encountered during field work than to make it all appear easy going and thereby encourage idle optimism. I intend, therefore, to devote a few more paragraphs to the preliminaries of field training, and here goes.

In the first place, no gun should be carried during early field training, and the chosen country should be fairly open, with a certain amount of game or rabbits, or both, thereon. Too much game will tend to over-excite the puppy, while the complete absence of scent will bore him stiff and be a complete waste of time. Do not expect your puppy to bound ahead at the first command and start quartering his ground like an old stager – he is far more likely to refuse to leave your side or, if he does do so, to stop and eat every piece of filth that he comes upon. A twenty-five-yard check cord can be worn by the puppy during his first outing or or two, particularly if he is of headstrong disposition. If, however, you are absolutely confident of his obedience (as you should be), I would suggest working him free at first, *only using the check cord if he blots his copybook*. Choose for the first outing a good scenting day with a slight breeze, and work upwind at first.

JUMPING

I like my dogs to be able to jump fences and other obstacles which are likely to be encountered during an ordinary day's shooting, and also to enter water willingly. These two assets are quite easily taught if you make a point of never helping the puppy over easy fences but walking on and calling him up. He will find a way through or over quick enough, and once he finds that he can jump without danger you will have no further trouble. Go out of your way to give this practice before you start him on field work, or he may develop into one of those miserable creatures who looks at his master and whines every time a fence is encountered. One of the most pleasing sights to the gundog lover is to see his faithful hound returning with his quarry in his mouth, gracefully leaping every obstacle encountered.

WATER WORK

Water training deserves careful attention, and here again it is very helpful to have a water-loving dog with you on the first occasion. A fine warm day should be chosen, and the puppy taken to a spot of shallow water where the bank shelves gradually.

I seat myself upon the bank and pretend that the last thing I desire is for my charge to get his feet wet, with the usual result that (like a child) he is soon paddling. Providing he evinces no strong dislike of going near the water, I amuse him (and myself) by throwing in sticks and stones to attract his attention. When he is interested I throw the dummy a few feet out into the water and ask him to fetch it. If he does so the distance is gradually increased until the puppy has to swim for it, but this does not usually occur on the first day. I end up by flinging the dummy on to the far bank, sending the pup across for it in due time. There are many variations of this exercise, and providing that care is taken not to force the rate of progress or frighten him in any way you can devise your own system.

We are often told that Labradors without exception love water, and that many spaniels are water-shy. This is just another fallacy which would be well dispelled. I find the proportion of water-loving Labradors no greater than that of spaniels, and if anything I have had more difficulty in coaxing Labradors into the water the first time. It must be admitted, however, that for work in water the Labrador's coat is much better, being denser and quicker drying than that of the spaniel, and that a water-loving Labrador is a joy to behold, especially for the wildfowler. Being stronger dogs they can better battle against heavy currents, but against this must be set the spaniel's wide and hairy feet, which must act as paddles far more efficiently than the 'cat' feet of the retriever. So there is really little to chose between the two breeds as far as average water-shooting is concerned.

A dog that seems really to dislike water must be coaxed with pieces of biscuit and be allowed to see a water-loving dog swimming about and enjoying himself. We read that one should on no account push or throw a dog into the water if he seems afraid of it, and in theory this is a very sound idea. I have been fortunate in that none of my pupils to date have refused to enter water under gentle persuasion, but after seeing others fling their reluctant dogs into water with perfectly satisfactory results and no permanent water-shyness, I do not think I should hesitate to use force as a last resort. I learned to swim myself by being pushed out of a dinghy by an impatient elder brother, and I shall be everlastingly grateful to him for his cruelty! Few dogs will refuse to enter water if a bird or rabbit be thrown in for them to fetch, but if this has to be resorted to it will have to wait until field work has been under way some time and they are accustomed to carrying fur and feather.

One point of interest in connection with water training which I have noted again and again concerns discipline at the water's edge. If the pupil has reached the stage of steadiness to a thrown dummy before being given water experience it is likely that the handler will make it sit on the bank and wait for orders before going into the water for the thrown dummy or piece of biscuit, whichever is being used. Now this can be a mistake, especially with a dog known to be averse to water, and I frequently find it very helpful (although from the purist's point of view unethical!) to throw my dummy and allow or even encourage the dog to run in straight away. The same principle sometimes applies to thick cover training, and my object is to get the dog into the disliked element almost before it has time to realize what is happening. In this way, natural energy and enthusiasm overcome caution or even nerves, and before it realizes what is happening the pupil is in cover or water and finding it not as bad as it expected – in fact, quite enjoyable and with something to fetch at the end of it.

Training, in all departments, must be flexible and individual circumstances and conditions taken into account. It is all very well to sit at a desk and theorize, writing that once a dog is steady to thrown dummies it must never thereafter be allowed to run in, let alone encouraged to do so. If circumstances appear to demand it, any experienced trainer will do the most unorthodox things in order to attain his object. True, once you have allowed a hitherto steady dog to run in, you are going to have a little difficulty in re-steadying it, but it can be done and, if the object is achieved (only when all else has failed), then there is no earthly reason why it should not be done. It probably all boils down to the question of knowing the individual pupil and judging just how far you can go in certain respects, but this, after all, is the main art of training. Indeed, unless you study the temperament of the individual pupil and really *know* it – and the pupil really knows *you* – then it is better not to attempt to train at all, but to pass the job on to somebody else. Not even the most experienced trainer is always right, and many a man has found that his judgement of a pupil's temperament has been at fault, but he can almost always make the necessary adjustments with ultimate success.

We are now all set to start field training proper. In the meantime, a little extra exercise on hard roads will be beneficial to your puppy for hardening the feet and muscles, and an increase of meat in the diet will help to prevent the additional waste of body tissue which will result from the added strain of hard work under service conditions.

STEADINESS TO FUR

There seems to be little doubt that steadiness to fur is one of the training tasks over which most difficulty is encountered, and this is hardly surprising when one considers that the main art in training is to keep a dog steady yet to retain his keenness to hunt.

In the next chapter I mention the rabbit pen method of training, which is widely adopted by those who have the necessary ground (and wire!). There is, however, another means by which a puppy can be accustomed to seeing fur and, more important still, learn to drop the moment the rabbit moves. I refer, of course, to the use of a tame rabbit, a practice which is not nearly so generally indulged in as might be supposed. Whether there is a suspicion that a certain amount of cruelty to the rabbit is involved, or if it is that few gundog men keep tame rabbits, I do not know, but I do know that with the aid of my old Flemish Giant doe, Mrs Mopp, I successfully trained a number of puppies to steadiness without having to make a wire pen.

The larger varieties of tame rabbits, especially the Flemish Giants, are not nearly so active as their smaller brethren, such as the Dutch variety. For this reason a Giant can often be trained to run about (or perhaps lop about would be an apter term) on an ordinary lawn without getting out of hand. As a rule they are docile creatures, easily caught and willingly handled.

The procedure is simplicity itself, and very definitely no cruelty to the rabbit is involved if certain precautions are observed. In the first place the rabbit should be allowed a daily spell of freedom on the lawn without the pupil being present in order to accustom him (the rabbit) to his future duties. Almost certainly he will enjoy nibbling the fresh grass, and will quickly learn to be picked up, handled and moved to various parts of the garden without complaint.

When the rabbit has been used to this sort of treatment long enough the puppy, firmly held on a check cord or lead, can be introduced to him. He can, if necessary, be pegged down while the rabbit is allowed to roam about, any movement on the part of the puppy being immediately checked. A few days of this, and the average young dog will learn to behave himself in the presence of the delectable fur.

One can then proceed further with the training, and the puppy may be allowed to go up to the rabbit, still held on his cord. The moment the rabbit moves off the puppy must be dropped, either by voice, whistle or the cord. It must be clearly emphasized that any undue display of harshness to the puppy at this juncture will, in all probability, completely ruin the effects of the lesson. His eagerness to hunt has got to be retained, the novel item being self-control which the trained gundog is expected to display in the presence of ground game. It is no earthly use to allow the puppy to rush up to the rabbit and then to check him with a blow and a sharp tug on the cord. Everything must be done in a deliberate and unhurried manner, all show of excitement or annoyance on the part of the trainer being avoided.

It is surprising how quickly an intelligent pup will cotton on to the idea of dropping the moment the rabbit moves, and once he has displayed sufficient reliability in this respect the check cord can be dispensed with, and the dog allowed to work loose. The command to drop can then be used to remind him of his duty, should he fail to go down as the rabbit moves. Training can be carried even further if you can allow the rabbit to roam about in the vegetable garden and encourage the puppy to seek, but always insist that the dog goes down the moment the rabbit moves himself. This is a stage nearer the real thing, and the cover of a cabbage patch can be surprisingly good for teaching a dog to use his nose and to quarter his ground. These lessons should, of course, be deferred until the pup is in an advanced stage of hand training and obedient to command, and (if used) whistle.

An interesting point in connection with the use of tame rabbits is the variability displayed by different members of the same breed. I have tried and discarded many rabbits in my time, and on the whole I find bucks more satisfactory than does for training purposes (Mrs Mopp was an exception) as the latter are liable to attack a young puppy with their hind legs, which might well put a puppy off fur for life. The rabbit must never be tired out, nor roughly handled, and any attempt to seize him by the dog must be prevented.

5

The pupil in the field

FIELD WORK

Your puppy's first day in the field is a great day, both for him and for yourself, and if your hand training has been thorough you will soon be receiving a just reward for all the spadework put in. Do not expect too much at first, and be prepared for several uneventful days and severe setbacks. It is wise to remember that at this stage of training many a promising puppy has been ruined by a slight mistake on the part of his handler.

Choose a fine, good scenting day for your first expedition, and carry no gun. As previously mentioned, a twenty-five-yard check cord can be carried for use in case of necessity, and the selected country should be fairly open and with a small stock of game. Send your puppy out with the accustomed signal and word of command to hunt ahead, and walk slowly, quartering your ground as you would wish your pupil to do. Should he attempt to get further away than twenty to twenty-five yards, check him with a short blast of the whistle and signal him to come closer. If you are lucky enough to spot a rabbit or a hare squatting in its seat, work the pup in that direction, and be ready to give the command to sit should he start to give chase. In most cases the pupil will watch his game go away, and you can either command him to sit, if he has not already done so, or be content (as I am) with his standing fast. Walk up to him and make a great fuss of him, but discourage him from following up the trail by working him in a new direction.

If by any unfortunate chance your pupil gave chase, ignoring your commands, rate him upon his return, but do nothing more severe, for at this impressionable stage we wish the puppy to get to love hunting, and any violence on the occasion of his first mistake will seriously impair his keenness. The check cord can now be attached, and the puppy hunted so that on the next flush he can be stopped short by treading on the cord. Half an hour of this work is quite sufficient for the first few days, especially if scent is lacking and game scarce.

It is quite probable that it will be several days before the puppy is interested in scent at all, and the work will then be most boring for the trainer. Perseverence, and if possible the example of a keen-hunting but steady old dog, will work wonders, and it would be very foolish either to give up the lessons or to decide to force the rate of progress and take out the gun. You are going to have the pleasure and happiness of shooting over your dog for many seasons to come, and you would never forgive yourself for spoiling his training for the sake of a few days with the gun. However, once the puppy does taste the delights of scent, you will have more difficulty in restraining him from hunting than from getting him to do so! This realization of scent is often a very sudden development – I have often been out with a pupil on one day when he did not seem to have any interest in hunting, and on the next day he was as keen as mustard. Again, that sudden unaccountable snapping in the brain!

There are many different opinions as to the right and wrong way of working a dog in the field. The general purpose dog is best trained to work, as far as possible, by signal alone, but this will only be obtained gradually and by experience – in the meantime, I recommend the double system of command and signal, gradually leaving out the commands as the puppy understands the meaning of the signals. Be sure that your signals are really distinct, and of course keep to the same ones. The same applies to the whistle, and if you can train your puppy to look for instructions by a chirp of the whistle, and come right in to a long blast, this is about all that is necessary.

Personal preference must play a big part in your method of working your dog. There are some people who religiously work their dogs according to the wind and make quite a fetish of always doing this. To my mind this is all wrong – my dogs have to work whichever way I desire, not according to the prevailing wind, which is seldom favourable, as roughshooters know too well. Quite apart from this, it is obviously foolish to get your dog used to working in one particular way in relation to the wind – if you do this when he is young he will later on be hopeless if you should have to work him in any other manner.

I have letters from time to time from self-styled experts, telling me the right and wrong way to work a dog in the field. Generally the writers are of extremely limited experience, but even so they are entitled to their views. But surely the right way to work a dog in the field depends upon the type of ground, type of dog, species of game and the position of the boundaries of the shoot. No hard and fast rules can be laid down about this, and therefore I say, teach your dog to work upwind, downwind and crosswind – do not handicap his whole future by getting him used to one method. This is a digression, I know, but to my mind an important one, which should be borne in mind from the start of field work.

Then there is the type of shooter who is constantly talking to his dog during work, making weird gesticulations and (he would have us believe) generally encouraging his dog. Do this by all means if it pleases your fancy, but it does not help your dog one iota, and it not only looks extremely foolish, but is most irritating to anyone accompanying you! A dog which is constantly talked to and waved at will gradually cease to take any notice of his master's absurd antics, or perhaps become so reliant upon them that he is unable to work without them.

It is an unfortunate fact (from a dog's point of view) that the majority of people think that they possess dog sense; tell them that they are in error and they see red! Not possessing dog sense is no crime in itself – very few people do – but the shame is that it is not admitted, and so they go on thinking they know, too proud or foolish to seek advice. The usual trouble is that the dog is given credit for more brains than he possesses, and if he does not understand a command or signal immediately is considered foolish. A man without dog sense, but with patience and common sense, who will try to see everything from the dog's point of view and not merely from his own, will make a better trainer and handler than the fellow with a certain amount of dog sense and a lot of conceit.

A few gunless weeks in the field with your puppy will be well repaid, and during this time do all you can to interest him in the scent of game. Encourage him to enter thick stuff, but on no account force him in, and do not at this stage let him hunt out of sight completely. If in his eagerness he gets too far ahead, check him at once and make him come in. The distance at which he is to work from you is a matter of personal taste, but the usual permissible maximum is about twenty-five yards. At a greater distance game would be out of shot before the gun could be brought to bear upon it, and the puppy would not be under such good control. If he persistently gets beyond this limit, the time-honoured check cord method takes a lot of beating, but I only advise using one in the field to correct chasing or if your puppy ignores your whistle, command and signs to come closer when hunting. If in his excitement he repeatedly ignores you, attach a twenty-five or thirty-foot check cord, and check him from ranging too far by standing on the end and tugging it to make him come in. As soon as he realizes that he is still under command even when hunting, dispense with the cord.

Much has been written about the ability of a dog to quarter his ground intelligently and, while he can be encouraged to this thoroughly, I do not consider that quartering can, strictly speaking, be taught; a natural instinct can be developed, and this is all that you are likely to be called upon to do. When the puppy is well out in front, attract his attention with a short whistle, and direct him to right or left. When he reaches the range limit check him again, signalling him to cross over to the other side. Most puppies soon respond to this signalling system, especially if they have been used to receiving commands by signal earlier. This is one of the advantages of my method, mentioned earlier, of making a dog sit and look at his supper until he is given the signal to get up and eat it. You may be sure he will get into the habit of watching your hands eagerly if this is always done. In the same way your puppy should from time to time have a certain small patch of cover pointed out to him, and be made to work that patch only. Frequently, when in the field, make your puppy drop for no apparent reason, just to practise him. Try to obtain obedience to the hand signal in this, too, because often when stalking wary game it is necessary to drop your dog silently. The earlier a puppy is used to hand signals the better, and to show what can be done in this direction I have at the time of writing a springer puppy who will sit when signalled to do so – and she is only nine weeks old!

If you find that your puppy is too full of good spirits and goes bounding about all over the place when first sent out to hunt, he should be given tiring exercise before being taken into the field. At all times it is desirable to walk the puppy to and from the shoot strictly at heel, and to give him spells of walking at heel in between field lessons, or he may become slack and keep breaking heel to sniff about, which is a most annoying habit and extremely difficult to cure once firmly established. Spaniels are always more trouble in this respect than retrievers, although the latter are by no means guiltless on occasion.

I mentioned above that correct quartering cannot be taught, but encouraged. One excellent method of encouraging is by appealing to the pupil's stomach! A few pieces of broken biscuit thrown to the right and left as you are walking, and the puppy will quickly learn to range from side to side, but I only recommend this in the case of puppy who will learn by no other way, as I consider tit-bits and feeding during lessons and work tend to take the pupil's mind off the real purpose of the instruction, and puppies come to expect continual edible encouragement if this is over-done!

The trainer of a no-slip retriever will not have to heed most of these early field lessons – rather will he have to discourage his pupil from noticing game and rabbits. For this purpose evening walks (with the pupil rigidly at heel) among game, checking any attempt to hunt, will be the best thing. The more temptation the retriever can be subjected to the better, providing that adequate means for checking him are at hand.

Many trainers use a wired-in enclosure containing live rabbits, wherein they first introduce their pupils to fur, but although this is undoubtedly useful and an excellent method of keeping young dogs under close observation and control, the average man will not readily have access to such an enclosure. It may take longer to obtain complete satisfaction from a puppy without resorting to these intensive methods, but there is a great deal to be said in favour of really natural training, and I prefer a dog trained under natural conditions so far as field work is concerned, always providing that the early obedience lessons have been thoroughly mastered.

The trainer's own nature is nearly always reflected in his dog, and thus we find that the puppy trained by a man of excitable temperament also becomes excitable, the stolid man's dog becoming sensibly stolid. Try, therefore, not to get excited when game is flushed, and do not rush about shouting at your pupil. It is a great help to the dog if, when a rabbit is sprung or a bird flushed, the trainer stops dead in his tracks and keeps his eye on his pupil, ever ready to check any attempt to chase, and to praise good behaviour.

When my young dogs have remained gloriously steady to a flush, I wait about half a minute and then go up to them and give them a good fussing and much praise. If they unfortunately start to give chase, but stop on command, they are taken back to their original position and rated sternly, being made to feel extremely small, and are kept on the drop for a considerable time. If they do not even stop chasing on command, my procedure varies with the age and experience of the dog. If it is a first offence, he is put back to hand training and dropping lessons, and if possible allowed to watch some tame rabbits in a run in the garden, being reproved if he tries to chase them or jump at the run. If, on the other hand, it is a dog who has had some previous field work and who has always performed well in the past, he is dragged back and scolded well thereafter wearing the check cord for the remainder of that lesson or, if no check cord is available, kept at heel and made to drop to the getaway of the next few rabbits. I only use a whip as a last resort, and then only if the dog knows just where he has erred, and will not become cowed.

Some time ago a correspondent stated, in effect, that it is useless to expect a young dog trained upon modern artificial lines in the early stages to perform like a field trial winner when taken into the field, and that he never used these methods, but started the puppy off on the real thing. It is unfortunately very true that many people expect their young dogs, whose hand training leaves nothing to be desired, to perform brilliantly when allowed into the field, not realizing that the change-over from artificial objects to real game can only be carried out gradually, and every effort must be made to ensure that the pupil realizes that what he learned to do with the dummy must henceforth be carried out with game. It is with this gradual change-over that I propose to deal now, but in passing it is worth remarking that I consider very few dogs could be taught from the beginning using real game, even given a trainer of exceptional understanding.

I am now assuming that our imaginary pupil has been given a

number of field days on the lines suggested, and that he has behaved himself and remained steady to the game which he has flushed or, if not, that disciplinary lessons are being given with the object of curing any faults. I shall enlarge upon these lessons some time in the future. In the meantime we shall accustom our puppy to carrying game for the first time (if no scent-trail lessons have been given).

My method is simply this, I procure a recently killed (but cold) rabbit (or, if the season permits, a partridge), and taking the puppy for a walk I suddenly produce the carcass, make the pupil sit and allow him to sniff the scent; then, calling him to heel, I walk on, dropping the carcass in full sight of him in the same way as the dummy was used during earlier lessons. When I am about twenty-five or thirty yards away from the rabbit, I send the puppy back for it, but continue to walk slowly, casting occasional backward glances to see what is happening. Usually these first lessons with real game are rather trying. Some puppies will pick up and carry by a piece of skin, dragging the carcass along the ground; others will nose and mouth the rabbit, turning it over but refusing to lift it, and a few will pick it up and rush off with it to a quiet corner, where they lie down and start tearing it to pieces. In the first case all promises well. The puppy has it in him and it is only a question of time before he finds it much easier to give the rabbit or bird a body grip, and so balance it across his jaws. The dog which refuses to lift is a bit of a problem, and (to take an extreme case) I will detail how I dealt with a yellow Labrador, which stubbornly refused to lift a dead rabbit for nearly an hour, although a good retriever of the dummy.

First, I called in my own experienced springer bitch, and making both dogs sit, sent her to retrieve it after the usual disciplinary interval. This I repeated several times, and then sent off my pupil. She bounced up to the rabbit with great eagerness, sniffed it, nosed it and returned looking sheepish. This happened twice, so I then altered my tactics, and casting economic consideration to the wind, I threw the rabbit a short distance. Still my Labrador would not pick it up, and once again my bitch had to do her schoolmistress stuff. All to no avail. After about half an hour of this, I gave the dogs a run round for about ten minutes, and then returned to the lesson. A few more trials convinced me that the Labrador was not going to learn from my bitch's good example, and so very gently I opened her mouth and placed the rabbit in; holding her jaws lightly closed with one hand and leading her with the other, I walked the Labrador a few yards, at the end of which I took the rabbit and made a great fuss of her, giving her pieces of biscuit and generally making her understand that she was being a good dog. Again I threw the rabbit and sent her out to it, and to my delight she actually picked it up gingerly, but almost immediately dropped it again and came back to heel. I repeated my previous tactics twice more, and on the third occasion I was rewarded for my patience, my pupil picking up and bringing in the rabbit like an old stager, holding it gently across the middle. I left it at that, deciding that she had now done what I wanted and would probably be all right in future, whereas any more attempts at the time might sicken her of a task on which she obviously was not too keen.

As I have said, this was an extreme case – usually the example on a few occasions of another dog retrieving will do the trick, and I do not recommend forcing a dog to carry except as a last resource – if you do have to do this you cannot be too gentle, if you would preserve a tender mouth in your pupil.

Now for the puppy who sits down and starts tearing at his rabbit. Call and whistle him to heel, running past him as you do so, and most likely he will get up and follow with it in his mouth. If so, take it from him gently whilst you are still walking. If this does not work, go up to him and lift him up bodily rather than pull the game from his mouth, when it will probably drop to the ground. If it does not you will have to take it from him, but whatever you do do not hurt the puppy in so doing, and do not tug and pull at the rabbit. Moreover, do not lose your temper and beat him; just trust to luck, time and the example of a good retriever to adjust his ideas of what should be done with game.

On no account should stale or badly damaged birds or rabbits be used for these lessons – the fresher the better. Pigeons I do not recommend, and certainly never domestic fowls. If a bird is used, it is advisable to tie the wings close to the body, and if a tame rabbit do not expect a small spaniel to lift a seven-pound Flemish Giant the first go-off. The reason I have given this lesson (which is really hand training) in the field work section is because we are on the eve of taking our pupil out shooting for the first time, and although you can have been giving scent-trail lessons for some while it is as well to have the experience of carrying and delivering the real thing, immediately prior to this, fresh in your pupil's mind; otherwise excitement might spoil everything on the day!

Readers may have noticed (probably with irritation!) that I am inclined to repeat myself throughout this book. This is quite intentional, for no other way can I stress the various important points which may make or mar your dog's education. My chief mission is to prevent others falling into the same mistakes that I myself made when I first started training, ruining a good dog in the process. But whereas I have had ample opportunity to learn from my sad experiences, the reader who may be training his first gundog will want to obtain good results from his first attempt. This is also the reason why I implore trainers to look at training from the psychological angle, and to realize that inattention to some small detail may quite possibly affect your dog's career.

Perhaps if I illustrate a typical first shooting lesson as given to my own dogs, the reader will get some idea how to proceed; not because I think my method a great deal better than anyone else's, but because I always carry out this lesson on ground holding a good few rabbits, but very little feathered game, which will most likely apply to your ground as well! I start off with my puppy at heel and take him to the most suitable cover for rabbits, wherein I can also keep a watch on his movements. Keeping him at heel, I try to find and put up a rabbit or game at which I fire a blank (or, if no blanks, fire wide to miss). The puppy, having been used to the gun fired near at hand, shows no fright and drops to the shot – if he does not do so he can be ordered to by voice, or left standing, whichever you prefer. I like to be quite sure that the puppy saw the rabbit, and after about a minute's pause I make a great fuss of him. This is repeated if possible and, provided that the puppy has remained steady, he is thereafter allowed out in front to hunt. Fire blank (or miss) the first head of game he puts up, and, if he has remained steady, be content and take him home. These lessons should be given for several days and are never wasted effort, because the all-important habit of steadiness is being ingrained under actual shooting conditions, whereas if you allow him to retrieve straight away the first head of game at which you fire, trouble quickly ensues.

After several lessons on these lines, I kill a rabbit or a bird which the puppy has put up and, making quite sure that it is stone dead and hidden in cover, or at any rate out of sight of the pupil, I send him off for it, walking off myself, with only an occasional backward glance to see what is going on. Directly I see that the puppy has the retrieve in his mouth (he having previously been shown that it is to be retrieved on the lines previously described) I call him up with the usual low whistle, and take the rabbit from him very gently. If his delivery is still bad (which I hope is not the case!) it must be taken whilst we are both still walking; if not, I stop and stroke his head whilst removing the rabbit, immediately putting it out of sight in the game bag.

Yes, it is as simple as this if (and what an if!) the conditions are right. By this I mean that the game must be stone dead and not badly shot and bloody, which will incline the puppy to stop and mouth it. The quarry must be right out of sight of the puppy when he is sent out to fetch, or he will quickly start running in to birds and rabbits. The more he has to hunt to find the body the better and, while he is doing so, for heaven's sake keep quiet and do not try to help him by signals and shouts. Simply give him the direction with the usual hand sign, and leave all else to the puppy's nose – he will learn a great deal more this way. Only if he starts casting about wildly in completely the wrong direction should he be interfered with, and then only recalled and sent out afresh in the right direction.

On no account should a puppy at this stage be sent for a wounded rabbit or bird; let him have some experience first, or the excitement of the chase may prove his (and your) undoing.

If you have rabbits to spare, and a good deal of time for training, there is a small refinement that is worth while. This is to shoot several rabbits over your dog and retrieve the first one or two yourself, keeping the puppy sitting meanwhile. After this, let him retrieve two out of every three rabbits you shoot, but not every one. This idea is solely to implant the habit of steadiness – let him think that every rabbit is for his attention and he will tend to become unsteady to shot.

When my pupil shows that he is getting the hang of things as a no-slip retriever, I repeat the programme, with him hunting up the game himself, always providing that he remains steady to shot.

I am assuming that you are training a dog for your own use,

and that is all being done in your limited spare time, It is, however, very useful to have someone with you to do the shooting on the first few days, so that you need not carry a gun and can concentrate on the dog. This is not absolutely essential, and I personally so dislike having anyone with me when training (unless they can keep their mouths shut and their eyes open – and how few can!) that I only do so in the case of a puppy which from one cause or another is giving trouble and needs my sole attention. There is, however, one little point that is interesting in connection with this. I have found that most puppies, if taken out alone at first, become exceedingly cunning when you do take someone shooting with you or go with a party. They imagine that your attention is distracted from them (which it all too often is!) and take advantage to the extent of breaking heel and doing a little self-hunting. Watch out for this when you first take your dog out in company, and let him see that he is still under control. All the more reason why your chosen assistant, if you want one, should be a sensible fellow and not interfere with you or the dog, but simply concentrate on shooting and leave you to concentrate on the dog.

My next section will deal with the retrieving of runners and sundry unpleasant accidents which may occur whilst out shooting with the puppy, most of which can be overcome by the application of common sense, patience, and a sense of humour!

RETRIEVING RUNNERS

An omission of mine has been to give the method of obtaining instant obedience to call, which I promised earlier to explain when the 'sit' was well learned. Well here it is, and I think you will find that used consistently and patiently this method will do much to improve a wayward dog's obedience. We will imagine that your dog is at some distance from you; you give him the signal, whistle, or word to come to heel and he disobeys. Immediately make him sit, walk up to him, put your hand on the top of his head and rate him; catch him by the throat and pull him several yards in the direction from which you came, drop him again, walk back to your former position and call him up. That is all there is to it – quite a well-known trick among dog trainers for which I claim no copyright, but which the average man may not know. The point is, of course, that the dog is made to understand just what he has done wrong, and were you to hit him (as do so many people) for disobeying when he did ultimately come to heel he would imagine he was being punished for coming in, not for disobeying you the first time. If such details of training were scrupulously attended to by every trainer, amateur and professional, the general standard of obedience would be much higher than it is today.

Readers will, I hope forgive me for this digression, and I will now get on with the original topic of this section – the retrieving of wounded game and runners. It depends largely how your dog has progressed in his field work when this becomes permissible, but once you are assured of his steadiness and his mouth, you can look forward to starting what is to me the most interesting work of all. If, like myself, you are a bad shot, your work will be made a lot easier – otherwise you may have to wait quite a time before you only wound a bird or rabbit! And here I am forced to give advice which goes very much against my better nature, that is if you wish to preserve your dog's steadiness.

The cardinal rule must be never, never send your young dog for a runner which is still in sight. Always wait until the quarry has passed out of sight and then put your dog on the scent, or assuredly he will be running into shot before many days if you send him straight away. Of course, once your dog is experienced (say about two or three years of age, depending upon the amount of work he has had) this precaution is not so necessary, but with a puppy it is vital. Nothing excites a young dog more than a rabbit dragging itself along on three legs, or a bird skimming down and running off. However, this is a matter for your personal taste and conscience, but as you have trained your dog to steadiness so far it would be foolish to ruin him now, and you can be consoled by the people who will tell you that a steady dog collects his game just as quickly as does the one who runs into shot, although it must be admitted that such has not been my experience. Let it be hoped that you will not have too many runners during your shooting career, and that your dog quickly becomes reliable and can be allowed more licence.

Another essential point in the retrieving of wounded game – do not become flurried yourself. Your reactions are reflected in your dog; show the least sign of excitement or eagerness yourself and your dog will become a whiner and start partially running in. If it is your desire to have a really reliable dog so far as tracking and retrieving wounded game is concerned, do not follow him up in his hunt, in the mistaken belief that you are helping him. He can tell by his nose things of which you, with your feeble olfactory nerves, could never be aware, and you will be doing more harm than good by giving him directions during his quest. Providing that he starts from the right spot, keeps his nose down and appears to be puzzling out the line, leave well alone. You can follow him the first time or two at a discreet distance (and out of sight if possible) and see how he carries on, checking him if he should break away after a rabbit which gets up in front of him, but as I have said, he will learn far more by being thrown upon his own initiative.

One or two very annoying things are liable to happen during the course of a day's shooting, especially at a party where guns are walking up game. Try, therefore, to give your dog his first few experiences of collecting runners while you are out alone with him. Remain at the spot whereon you first gave him the scent, and make a great fuss of him when he returns with his quarry. I know of no greater happiness than when my dog brings to hand a wounded bird or rabbit, after puzzling out a difficult line through a well-stocked wood, and the first day this happens to you will indeed be a great occasion.

PICKING UP AND BEATING

One of the most useful and effective media whereby the gundog pupil can be given advanced experience under ideal conditions, especially early in its first season, is often ignored by owner-trainers. I refer to picking up at big shoots, where the handler does not carry a gun but confines himself to dog handling, and is thus enabled to concentrate upon his pupil whilst someone else worries about the shooting. Serious trainers, both amateur and professional, find that picking up on organized shoots provides ideal work and experience for their dogs – be they spaniels or retrievers.

Although it is not alway easy to find suitable shoots whereon pickers-up are welcome, I have found that a tactful approach to estate proprietors, syndicate shoots and, particularly, gamekeepers will usually achieve the desired end and, providing that you have a reasonably controllable and efficient dog, your assistance on shooting days will be welcome. The picker-up is enabled to give his dog retrieving experience on different types of game and can usually arrange for all sorts of situations to meet the requirements of his training programme. On the average big shoot he can give his dogs birds lying in easy places and also quite difficult runners or dead birds hidden by thick cover. He will also be able to put his dog under severe temptation while in a position to control it – from birds falling close by on open ground at a drive to hares and rabbits getting up under the dog's nose while it is walking up.

This sort of work is valuable to any retrieving gundog, be it spaniel, retriever or pointer-retriever. The man who is training a dog for general roughshooting, which calls for much questing in search of unshot game, can and should cash in on the present demand for, and shortage of, beaters for driven shoots. Contact a gamekeeper or shoot proprietor and offer your services as a beater-cum-picker-up. In this way you will have ideal opportunities to work your dog as a quester in all types of cover, in company (a most important point), to put it under varying temptations and still give it some retrieving practice at the conclusion of the drives.

To obtain picking up or beating on a good shoot – and these days there are good shoots in almost all country areas – I suggest that the best initial approach is via the headkeeper (unless you know personally the estate proprietor or syndicate leader). In the first place you must convince him of your enthusiasm for the job; of your honesty and, above all, that your dog is not liable to do more harm than good on a shooting day! Tact, and proof that you have a good appreciation of the underlying principles of shooting and sportsmanship, will go a long way towards securing the goodwill of the man who matters.

On a shooting day, put yourself unreservedly in the hands of the headkeeper or shoot leader. Do as you are told, go and stop where you are directed, do everything to further the interests of the shoot and avoid, at all costs, upsetting the individual guns (or beaters for that matter) by tactless remarks or criticisms. Control your dog in such a way that not only is training advanced but the shooting is not spoiled. Do not hesitate to use a lead (or even the check cord) if it appears to be necessary in order to keep your dog under control, both during and between drives. In this way, and providing that your dog performs reasonably well, you will quickly find that not only are you welcome at such shoots, but that you (or perhaps I should say your dog) are in demand!

PIGEON SHOOTING

Pigeon shooting in its various forms can provide valuable education and practice for a dog which is at field work stage, all the more so because of the comparative availability of pigeon shooting in most country areas, where farmers usually welcome the genuine sportsman who will help to reduce their number one enemy. As with obtaining picking up, a tactful approach is essential and it will probably be necessary to convince any farmer or landowner of your trustworthiness and sense of sportsmanship. If a farmer is good enough to grant permission for pigeon shooting only, it is the height of folly to raise your gun to anything else. In other words, do not poach!

Pigeon shooting from a hide over decoys, flighting at dawn or dusk, or stalking the hedgerows and woods can all provide work, albeit of a somewhat specialized nature, for your dog, but a word of warning is very necessary. Woodpigeons are notoriously loose-feathered and are often disliked for this reason by many young dogs until they have had some sensible experience of them. For this reason, my advice is that *before any dog is allowed to retrieve a freshly shot pigeon it should have had practice at home on cold birds shot a day or two previously*. Failure to carry out this very necessary precaution has frequently ended in a promising youngster being ruined – either biting its bird or perhaps refusing to touch them at all. Cold pigeons shot on the previous day are much more tightly feathered than the warm article and, if used a time or two in similar manner to the dummy (thrown, hidden or dropped, and dog sent back for them) should quickly give confidence to your pupil and prepare him for more advanced work.

Hide work is particularly valuable experience for any dog likely to be used for duck flighting or driven game shooting, and provides practice not only in retrieving but patience and quietness during the lulls plus, of course, in marking falls and use of nose, especially where birds fall in cover. Do not let your dog retrieve every bird shot, and never send it for a wounded bird until it is perfectly reliable on stone-dead ones.

6

Common problems

TRAINING

Many and varied are the problems which crop up for dog owners in general, and gundog trainers in particular, on which they seek instant advice, often to be disappointed! No one book can possibly hope to deal with *all* the contingencies which may arise, but at the end of this chapter I have included, in simple question-and-answer form, my advice on some of the most common queries which have been thrown at me over the years, either in letters from readers, after lectures and talks I have given up and down the country, or at quiz sessions on gundog training and management.

Questions on management are usually straightforward and comparatively simple to answer. Those upon training tend to be much more complex and involved, and the solutions suggested cannot be guaranteed to work in every case, because no two dogs are exactly alike in temperament and without first-hand experience of the individual concerned it is difficult to do more than generalize. What suits one dog and one handler may not suit another couple, but trainers must always be prepared to experiment and to use their common sense, adapting suggested methods and techniques to suit themselves and their pupils.

However, having written this, I cannot emphasize too strongly the wisdom of obtaining expert assistance and personal, practical help from an experienced trainer if you really find yourself up a gum tree on a particularly knotty problem. If you are really in trouble, seek out a good man (or woman), either an established professional trainer or an experienced amateur, rather than risk ruining your dog for all time, which is so easy to do if you give it the wrong impression by applying incorrect techniques or, more probably, by losing your temper with it. The gundog fraternity is well-known for its sportsmanship and willingness to assist the novice trainer if approached in a tactful manner and with due humility and the obvious desire to learn!

It has been said that there is no such thing as a bad dog – only bad owners! This is not strictly correct, because in all breeds of dog the odd untrainable rogue and the complete idiot crop up from time to time. Not only this, but gundog owners sometimes find themselves knocking their heads against a brick wall by trying to educate a dog of unsuitable breeding, from the working point of view; they would be well advised to part with it and start all over again with a puppy of impeccable pedigree and working background. That old saw, 'You cannot make a silk purse out of a sow's ear,' is particularly applicable to working gundogs, which *must* be bred for the job in hand.

Dogs vary to an amazing degree in their aptitude for hunting-up game, and this leads to a certain amount of worry on the part of the novice trainer. 'Why', I am sometimes asked, 'will my six-months-old puppy not go out and hunt for rabbits, etc., when my friend's spaniel puppy who is only five months old does so like an old stager?'

Natural ability or otherwise plays a great part in this hunting-up question, and of course the opportunities that the youngster has been given to nose scents and become interested in rabbits must also be taken into account. It is a great thing to be able to take a young puppy for walks over game-holding ground and to allow him to nose scents, but of course care must be taken that he does not flush and chase rabbits before he has become obedient and been given lessons in steadiness.

The rabbit pen is a great asset in many respects and, apart from using it for steadiness work, it can also be utilized to give the puppy something in which to scent about, after the rabbit has been removed. Indeed, most puppies which are undergoing the sort of training course to which I so often refer become interested in hunting whilst undergoing their steadiness lessons – if they did not there would be no object in trying to steady them! Occasionally a young puppy is taken into the rabbit pen and allowed to have a good hunt and chase after the rabbit (which I term the hunting-first method of training), and in this way he learns to enter cover and to get keen on hunting. These are the two obvious advantages of this system of training.

However the puppy is being trained, one youngster will be found to take a keen delight in hunting and entering cover, running scents and flushing game at four or five months of age, while another will not do so until he is eight, nine or even ten months old. It is usually possible to tell at a much younger age if the puppy is naturally gifted or liable to become what I term a dope – a lethargic and unresponsive animal without enthusiasm for his work. If, for instance, the pupil is a keen and quick retriever, and generally lively and responsive, then there need not be much fear of his becoming a dope, but even so he may be slow in getting into his stride so far as hunting game is concerned. No two dogs are alike, and the very precocious ones who will hunt at an early age need a longer course or discipline, whereas the more docile animal who is slower getting down to work can safely be introduced to game at an earlier stage of training, provided that he is fairly obedient.

One of the surest ways of boring a pupil and tending to make him slow and disinterested in game is to work him too long and too often on ground holding little or no scent, or on a very hot day. When a puppy gets to the field work stage of training he does not need to be worked every day, unless he is exceptionally keen. The training days and the ground to be traversed should be carefully chosen in order to ensure that there will be scent lying about, if not game and rabbits, according to the stage of training reached. But to go on for long spells encouraging the dog to hunt where there is no scent lying about will quickly tire the puppy and will defeat its own object.

Puppies from good working stock, be they retrievers or spaniels, pointers or setters, will rarely turn out to be non-hunters. There are, of course, exceptions to every rule, and there are liable to be exceptional pups in every litter, but only once have I experienced a complete dope from a litter of working and field trial spaniels, and he had not one atom of keenness about him. Why, I do not know. His brothers and sisters were outstandingly brilliant, and I have two in my kennel now who are a pleasure to work.

To encourage a dull puppy to hunt, I suggest that everything is done to stimulate interest in game, from allowing a mild chase in the rabbit pen at an early age (providing you are prepared to spend a little more time on steadying him later), to walks traversing game-holding cover. Above all, do not tire and bore the puppy by working him too long and too often on scentless ground – twice or thrice a week is quite sufficient, and spells of from ten minutes to half an hour to start with. Do not become discouraged if the puppy is a little slow coming to it – the chances are that by the time he has reached the age of nine months and has had the opportunity of flushing a rabbit or two the pendulum will swing in the other direction, and you will have difficulty in resstraining him from hunting! Watch him closely, in case you are handling a hopeless dog, but if he is lively and keen you have not much to fear.

On thinking back upon past training expeditions, there is no doubt in my mind that my patience has been most strained during field work, and particularly after my dogs have had a few retrieves of real game. The events during hand training can be controlled to a certain extent, but during a shooting expedition over a young dog all sorts of things are liable to happen. Here the man who has access to a wired enclosure containing a few live rabbits (living naturally) is at a great advantage over the average owner-trainer, but in any event these trying incidents have got to happen at some period during the dog's education, and so, like measles in a child, it is just as well to get it over early!

Directly a dog has tasted (not in the literal sense, let it be hoped!) real game, he is naturally made more keen, with consequent inclination to unsteadiness. Also, the connection between a shot and something to fetch is gradually dawning upon him. The general-purpose dog owner is at a disadvantage now compared with the no-slip retriever man, because it is very much easier to control the movements of a dog at heel than one hunting, say, twenty-five yards ahead. Prevention is better than cure, and the necessity for constant vigilance while the dog is hunting ahead must be strongly impressed upon the trainer. How many times have I stopped to light my pipe at the very minute that my dog has flushed a rabbit and, sensing that my attention was momentarily distracted from him, started to chase! How it is I do not know, but take your eyes from a young dog for but a few moments and he seems aware of it, and evil ensues. Watch your dog like a hawk, is my advice at this stage, and be ready to drop him by voice if he shows any inclination towards unsteadiness.

Then there is the temptation to hunt him in very thick cover out of sight – a very unwise thing to do at such an early stage of training. Of course, some dogs will retain a sense of obedience and discipline even when out of sight, but it is not advisable to take this for granted. Time enough to hunt him right out of sight when you are assured of his reactions to game flushed under your eyes. Well I know the temptation at this time! 'Dan has been pretty steady up to now, and time's getting on – I might just as well let him hunt that copse while I wait outside. He won't go wrong.' Yes, it has happened to me, many times. And each time I allowed my eagerness to get the better of me I dearly regretted it, and promised myself, 'Never again.'

But the reader will want to know what to do if his dog does break out even though, strictly speaking, you asked for it – and got it! Well, what can you do when your dog has run riot in, let us say, a small copse, refused to come back to your whistle and, although you have not the evidence of your eyes to go on, given chase to something that he found? Beat him when he comes back and he will be even more reluctant to come to heel in future. Let him get away with it and he will imagine that he has done just what you wanted, and will repeat the performance again at the earliest opportunity. The only thing that I can suggest is that you go back into the copse with him; ten to one he will lead you to the spot where he found his bird or rabbit. If you can be fairly certain of this, make him drop there, rate him in a stern voice, put your hand on his shoulders, look him straight in the eyes and scold him optically. Then return to your original position outside the copse and, after a pause, whistle him up again. In all probability he will immediately come bouncing back to you and, even if he is not aware that he was punished for hunting and chasing while out of sight, at least you have given him a useful lesson in instant obedience.

Now what about a right and left into a covey of partridges, the first being a runner, and the second a dead bird? If your dog remained steady he is almost certain to go for the last (and dead) bird first, whereas you will want him to gather the runner as quickly as possible. The only thing to do is to walk him to the fall of the runner, give him the line and let him retrieve the dead bird (unless it lies in the open) when he has duly gathered the runner. With experience a dog learns to gather runners first, no matter which fell first, but until he attains an age of discretion and shows by his general demeanour that he is becoming wise in the way of things, the only plan is to walk him to the fall. When only one bird has fallen this will not be necessary after a time, and he will soon learn to mark birds down at a considerable distance.

One of the most exasperating happenings is when your dog is on his way out to collect a bird or rabbit, and another rabbit jumps up out of his seat under the dog's very nose. Bet your life he will give chase, or at any rate start to until you call him off. Just another reason why he should be worked where game is not too abundant during the early stages. If this does happen, recall him, scold him and put him out afresh, clearly indicating the direction of the fall. If you have got your dog under such good command that, when he does by accident start a chase, you can call him to a halt instantly, you have little to worry about. Experience and constant checking will soon make him understand that he must keep to the business in hand and not go off on mad hunts. It can now be clearly seen (if it was not before) why the sitting lesson should have been thoroughly drilled into your pupil. If you have a dog, no matter how headstrong, who from early puppyhood has learned to drop sharply to command, half your worries are over. The drop is really the crux of the whole training, and for this reason it should be practised regularly even when your dog is not at work. If he becomes slack, or through your absence or some other cause shows reluctance to drop smartly to command and signal, stand no nonsense. Take him out with the check cord and when he is hunting ahead give the word of command, standing on the cord at the same time. An old remedy, but still one of the most effective!

The number of things which may crop up when training a young dog is so great that I cannot hope to deal with them all here, but I am trying to mention the most common, together with the best remedy for the faults. It must be stressed that no young dog should be taken to a shooting party until he is reliable, or the effect of the barrage of firing will be disastrous. However, after you have had your pupil out a number of times you will have some idea of his reactions to shooting, and you can gradually subject him to greater temptation by taking a friend or two out with you; the consequent extra amount of firing and noise will enable you to spot any weaknesses in his training.

One of the most trying things that is likely to come to your notice at this juncture is the inclination on the part of the puppy to whine and even yelp with excitement during and after several shots, if he is not permitted out to retrieve. This unpleasant habit is mostly developed by spaniels when they are used as no-slip retrievers after having been used to hunting ahead all the while. I have suffered from this many times, and I have been unable to discover any gentle psychological cure (I should be glad if anyone could tell me of one!) but I have managed to curb the habit by judicious application of a whip or lead at the right moment. The dog realizes that he is being punished for his noise if a cut is delivered after every whine, and soon learns that discretion is the better part of valour and keeps a discreet tongue in his head! The very nervy or excitable dog is more of a problem, as the whip will only make him more jumpy and nervy. In this case you can only grip his nose and scold him every time he utters the offending whine, and try to make him see that silence is golden. The subject is a very delicate one, for the whining dog shows great keenness for work and it is not desirable to cow him by harshness. Apart from this it is difficult, as well I know, to punish a dog effectively in public, as the other guns (probably, alas, quite disinterested in dogs) think you are being unnecessarily cruel, and frequently say so in no uncertain terms. However, there is no need for cruelty or excessive leatherings and, as in many other things, it pays to ignore public opinion and go your own way. If, however, you can eradicate this fault in the family circle, so to speak, so much the better. Of course the whole training course which I have outlined is intended to bring the dog up as far as possible artificially and without the excitement of game in the early stages, and the trainer who follows this plan will be far less likely to be bothered with an excitable dog than the one who has introduced his pupil to game prematurely. Far better, then, to give your puppy his first season in home waters until he has acquired a certain amount of control and experience.

A piece of advice that I should have tendered earlier is that the general-purpose dog will benefit by being worked as much as possible during his first season as a no-slip retriever. By acting thus you will help to impress your dominance upon him, and he will be all the steadier for the experience. Once you are assured that your pupil knows his job as a hunter-up of game, keep him at heel for the next few weeks, however great may be the temptation to work him; otherwise the bag might benefit but the training certainly will not.

A young dog, which has just completed his training is very easily spoiled, as I found to my cost last winter. Being forced to spend a few days in bed, I accepted the offer of a friend to exercise some of my dogs. I was under the impression that this pal knew his onions where dogs were concerned, but to my disgust I discovered a few days later that a very promising springer bitch was inclined to chase fur, although previously she had been rock steady. Upon enquiry I learned that my Good Samaritan had hunted this bitch and had actually encouraged her to follow a rabbit which she put up! I blame myself for permitting anyone else to take her out, but it just shows that you cannot be too careful in these matters.

In this case I had a long spell of hard work to win back the bitch to complete steadiness, and my method was to hunt her in long grass where I expected to find rabbits sitting out, keeping fairly close to her and checking any signs of unsteadiness. I used a check cord at first to give her one or two nasty falls, and thereafter relied upon the word 'No' to prevent chase. The drawback was that the high grass often prevented her from seeing the rabbit away, and many afternoons she flushed four or five rabbits without chasing or attempting to chase one – because she did not see them! In connection with this illustration of the ease with which a dog can be spoiled by mishandling, it should be remembered that when hunting a dog on rabbits it should always be worked in a fresh direction after the getaway, or it will be inclined to follow up the line, which in itself induces unsteadiness.

Giving chase must not be confused with eagerness to mark, and very many steady dogs will rush forward a few yards after a flush, especially if working in thick cover, in order to mark the fall. Strictly speaking, of course, the dog should have dropped to shot and remained steady, but over-eagerness is not always a bad thing, and each case must be judged on its merits and will depend upon the type of work you do. This movement to mark would probably be penalized at a field trial unless the judge was very discriminating, but I prefer (in the case of my dogs) to let the dog use his initiative in the matter, and only punish him for moving if it is obviously a flagrant case of unsteadiness. A good marker will save a great deal of time for the practical shooting man, and it is impossible to have it both ways. This is one of the several reasons why field trial dogs are not always the best for ordinary shooting, and vice versa.

GUNSHYNESS AND GUN-NERVOUSNESS

Several readers have written regarding alleged gunshyness in their dogs, and asking for advice. A typical letter runs as follows: '. . . I now have a fine golden Labrador, nine months old. He has not been out shooting yet but has passed through all the hand training stages. Is intelligent, has an excellent nose, and is obedient to all signals and commands. He has, however, shown signs of gunshyness (nervousness?). To train pups, I fire blanks with very little powder. A shot or two was tried at some distance away when he was six months old, but as he showed signs of fear I left it alone until last week. He does not seem to be any better, however, and shows reluctance to follow when I have the gun with me. I have had a gunshy dog before, but not one just like this. If I drop him and fire a shot he runs to me and gets between my legs. The dog is from grand working parents. The point is, is he worth going on with, or shall I spend all next summer messing about and then find I have a gunshy dog? We have a little shoot on the 22nd, to try and break up some untouched coveys, and I thought about giving him a try out for good or bad. There will be other dogs there and there will not be a lot of shooting. What do you say, chum?'

This I have quoted in full in order that I may grapple with the subject in some detail. The writer previously explains that he has always trained his own dogs and has 'been noted among friends for good (the best), steady, game-finding animals'.

To deal with this particular reader's problem before I generalize, I must say that he appears to have been most unwise. He tells us that his dog passed through all the hand training stages, but he neglects the most important of all (or rather shelves it until later), the training to gunfire. A nervous dog should on no account be left in that state, but taken in hand right away and cured, if possible. Otherwise, all further training is merely a waste of time and money.

In the first place it would be as well to differentiate between gunshyness proper and gun-nervousness. The former is almost hopeless, the latter usually curable. A gunshy dog shows abject terror at a shot, will run away and hide himself, and generally appear a nervous wreck. A gun-nervous specimen will show alarm, be startled by the shot, and perhaps run off in fear a little way, but he quickly recovers his composure, and does not exhibit such terror. The best plan with a young puppy is to test for nervousness with a sudden clap of the hands when he is not looking, and if he shows any nervous reaction put him on a special course of treatment. A gunshy dog should be discarded and, as the fault is believed to be hereditary (although it may skip a generation and then only appear in one or two members of a litter), it should certainly not be bred from.

Gun-nervousness frequently results from faulty early training, and flourishing the weapon will often cause it. Some men even use the gun as a convenient instrument of correction, which will implant a dread of it if nothing else does. Sometimes a man will assume that his pup will be all right on the day if he takes no notice of a few distant shots now and then, and therefore neglects any further training in this respect. A dog must be accustomed to seeing the gun flourished by the trainer before he ever hears it, and it should be thrown up into the firing position and swung round in a realistic manner while the pup is on the drop at a distance.

A dog which shows alarm at a distant shot but does not bolt in terror may safely be assumed to be gun-nervous only, and a useful method of allaying his fear is to have a gun fired at a distance just as he is being fed. He will in all probability quickly connect the firing with something pleasant! As his fear decreases, firing can be done at diminishing distances until ultimately he will allow the gun to be used under his very nose.

The presence of a hardened dog who does not object to gunfire is also a valuable aid to a nervous puppy, and this should be tried if possible. On no account should the pace be forced. If it is impossible to arrange for a firing session as suggested above, through the lack of assistance, the pupil can be started off by loud clapping of the hands when he is feeding, or the banging of a tin tray at a distance, although it is far better for his master to be beside him and for someone else to create the din. Another useful wrinkle is to allow the puppy to indulge in a chasing, and to fire

ntroduction to the real thing. First sniff of a freshly shot but cold and clean young abbit, which will be used like a dummy on the first few occasions

uccess achieved – a balanced hold of the rabbit and delivering right up to hand

Every gundog should learn to jump cleanly

Above: This type of fence can be very hazardous to an inexperienced dog unless there is a solid top rail, which here has been removed and can be seen lying on the ground

Returning over the same fence, encouraged by the recall whistle. Note the trainer's use of hand signals in both exercises

Questing practice

Above: Casting out with a clear hand signal

Nose well down on a scent

Encouraging into cover

The dummy-launcher is invaluable for giving a youngster experience of mild gunfire. This will teach the dog to mark accurately. Note that here the dummy is not fully seated on the spigot for the first lessons, so that it will not be ejected too far

a shot whilst he is in full cry after a rabbit. Again, there will be the connection between something pleasant and the gun, and he can, after all, be won back to steadiness, whereas fear of the gun will render any dog useless to the sportsman. All harshness whilst training a puppy to gunfire should be avoided, and after each explosion he should be made much of and given an edible reward, if none of the above methods are adopted.

QUESTIONS AND ANSWERS

WHAT BREED OF GUNDOG?

I have just taken up shooting, at the age of nineteen, and am very keen to acquire a gundog to train myself. My shooting is a mixture of very rough and driven game, and I cannot decide which breed of dog would suit my purpose best. I have no preconceived ideas, and am open to suggestions, but am under some pressure from my parents, with whom I live, to get a dog which is easy to train and manage. What are your thoughts about this?

As you have only just taken up shooting, and have no preconceived ideas as regards breed, the field is wide open to you! Your final choice should depend upon which type of shooting you will *mostly* indulge in because, quite frankly, the *perfect* all-rounder just does not exist. I think it would be well worth while for you to read up the whole subject, and you will find a description of every available breed of gundog, and their suitability for different forms of shooting, in *The Complete Book of Gundogs in Britain*, edited by Tony Jackson and published by Barrie and Jenkins. My own book, *Gundogs: Training and Field Trials*, should also prove helpful in making the correct decision, and comprehensively covers the training and management of all breeds.

AGE TO COMMENCE TRAINING

I have an English springer puppy three months of age, and have made up my mind to train him thoroughly. Is he too young to start on sitting, remaining on the drop, to come when called, minor retrieving and lead work, and water enjoyment? Will I kill his flair for speed by starting him young? My lessons at the moment last only about ten minutes, during a long walk over rough country, when I let him take to quite tough cover by following me I have your book on gundog training.

Three months is much too young to start your puppy's intensive course of training although, of course, you can encourage retrieving and delivery of a small dummy, teach lead walking, and introduce him to rough cover *in small doses*. You must, at all costs, avoid tiring and boring the puppy, and most definitely *not* yet start him on sitting and staying for long periods. I should also suggest that introduction to water be delayed for a few months, until the puppy is older and the weather (and the water) warmer. If you read my book thoroughly you will find most of this explained, and I feel sure that if you join a spaniel training club both you and your puppy will benefit considerably, not only from the discussion of various problems with other members, but from the practical demonstrations and advice given by the instructors and visiting top professional trainers at their periodical training sessions.

INDIFFERENT DELIVERY

I am very tempted to purchase from a friend a Labrador dog which is a brilliant gamefinder and reasonably steady. However, it has one fault that I should like to overcome: instead of bringing game straight to hand it circles the handler and often drops the retrieve out of reach. Can you suggest the reason for this and a possible cure?

I strongly suspect that this dog has at some time been punished (probably for running in) upon its return with the retrieve. This is one of the cardinal sins of handling; no dog should be punished upon returning to you for something that it did wrong previously, because it invariably associates the punishment with its very last action, and therefore gains completely the wrong impression and will in future be even more reluctant to come to hand. It is not easy to eradicate this false impression, but it should be possible with time and tact if it is not too firmly ingrained. Walk away (or even run away) as the dog returns with its retrieve, encouraging it by voice and/or whistle to come beside you, and then take the retrieve while you are both still on the move. Make a great fuss of the dog and, if using a dummy, even return it to the dog to carry walking beside you; every so often bending down, gently remove the dummy and praise the dog again. This practice can be conducted with the dog on the lead if necessary. One tip that I learned many years ago from Richard Sharpe – never, on any account, stare at a dog when it is bringing in its retrieve, but bend down in the receptive position and avert your gaze, encouraging it by voice or whistle meanwhile, once you have discontinued the walking-away practice.

HARD MOUTH

My two-year-old Labrador has a tendency to hard mouth, and damaged a few birds at the end of last season as well as some already this year. He is of impeccable working breeding, so that I doubt if it is an inbred fault, and he has never been chastised to make him bite from fear. The trouble seems to be due to his excitability and over-enthusiasm, especially when first winding the retrieve and snatching up the game. Also, on occasions, he grips too tightly when I am taking a bird from him. Is there any hope of a cure, and would it be a waste of time and money to enter him for trials, even though he is excellent in all other respects?

Hard mouth in a gundog is major fault, usually but not always hereditary and, once firmly ingrained, impossible to cure. Generally speaking, it is senseless to enter for trials a dog which *may* bite game, even though you could be lucky from time to time. Most judges, quite rightly, after consultation with their colleagues, eliminate from the stake any dog which bites game, however good it may be in other respects. In your case, as the dog is still young and comparatively inexperienced, it may be worth running him on for a few weeks and seeing if further experience will settle him down, as youngsters do sometimes damage their retrieves due to excitability. But I would be wrong to give you false hopes, and hard mouth is liable to get worse rather than better with age. It can be caused by giving a youngster real game to retrieve before it is ready for it, or through being spurred by a lively wounded cock pheasant. Modern trainers have little faith in old-fashioned so-called cures, such as covering a dead bird with a hedgehog skin or spiking it with wire or nails, and the man who could come up with a genuine remedy would make a fortune!

BEST TYPE OF WHISTLE

What is the best type of whistle to use on gundogs? I am somewhat confused by the multiplicity of patterns available, and by the conflicting advice of local experts. I have been told that the Acme 'Silent' whistle is the most effective, and that dogs respond to it automatically.

I doubt if there is such a thing as the 'best' type of whistle, and I can state quite categorically that, whatever pattern you select, your dogs must be *taught* to respond to it. I have a very high regard for the Acme 'Silent' whistle, to which most dogs respond well when it is tuned to almost any pitch, but the manufacturers are the first to point out that it is not a magic instrument. Probably the majority of professional gundog trainers would plump for the high-pitched staghorn or plastic whistle, with or without the pea, while my favourite (and that of the great majority of American trainers, incidentally) is the small Acme 'Thunderer' in plastic. This has many advantages, which include a large aperture which does not easily become blocked, great versatility of volume according to how it is blown, ready availability in most sports goods shops, and a reasonable price. It comes in a range of colours, which is useful because if you choose a bright one it can more easily be found if dropped in cover! Incidentally, always attach your whistle to a lanyard round your neck, and never carry it loose in your pocket, where it may become blocked and from which it can easily be dropped. Finally, a staghorn or plastic whistle has one very great advantage over a metal one, in that during very cold weather it does not freeze to your lips!

FEAR OF THUNDER

My two cocker puppies (which come of genuine working stock, I might add!) are scared stiff of thunder, and nearly go through the roof during a storm. They are just five months old and, although their basic training has been started, they have not yet been subjected to gunfire. Do you consider that they will prove to be gunshy and that I should get rid of them immediately and start all over again with pups from a different strain?

Thunder-shyness does not necessarily mean that your pups will prove gunshy. I have known many pups – and even adults – who went almost berserk in storms (and, during the war, at the sound of AA fire bombs), but were completely confident about gunfire; I have also known the reverse. Thunder-shyness is something out of which pups often grow, especially if you can be with, and pacify, them at the critical time. You could also give them tranquillizing tablets (obtainable from veterinary surgeons) to calm them down during thunderstorms but, of course, if you are away from home at the time neither of these suggestions is going to be of any help! However, I should not despair yet, but run your cockers on for a few weeks and *tactfully* introduce the sound of gunfire, preferably starting with the ubiquitous dummy-launcher, as this creates additional interest for the pupil, who watches and marks the lofted dummy. It occurs to me that you are starting your basic training quite early enough, and it may pay off to ease up on discipline for a period, otherwise the pups may become inhibited, especially as they are obviously of sensitive disposition.

SITTING AT A DISTANCE

I am having difficulty in making my Labrador puppy sit at a distance. She will sit immediately on command or whistle when by my side, on or off the lead, but will not do so when a few yards distant. She will sit indefinitely if I walk away from her, even if I go out of sight, and returns immediately upon command. Suggestions, please.

As your puppy is reliable on the stay, it should be comparatively simple to teach her to sit at a distance. My method is to sit the dog, walk away for twenty yards or so and call (or whistle) it in; when it is almost up to you, give the sit command. Repeat this a few times, and then start giving the command a little sooner, when the pupil is some yards away. Repeating this exercise, and giving the appropriate command and/or whistle and signal earlier and earlier (moving forward yourself and insisting upon obedience should the command be ignored), it should soon be possible to stop the dog at any point between yourself and where it was originally seated. Once the penny has dropped, you will find that the dog will respond to the sit command whether it is going away from or coming towards you. At all times be firm (but also tactful!), making your pupil realize that to hear is to obey.

FORCE RETRIEVING

My ten-months-old Labrador is an excellent retriever of the dummy, but refuses to lift the real thing. Do you consider that it should be given a course of force retrieving and, if so, how do I set about it?

In common with many of my colleagues, I deprecate forced retrieving unless all else fails. Not only is it a very specialized and backbreaking job, which if not properly carried out can lead to serious trouble between master and dog, but I believe that our gundogs should retrieve naturally and for the love of it, and the last thing we want to do is to perpetuate a fault of this nature by masking it and breeding from animals which have it. However, your puppy is obviously a natural retriever as it will carry the dummy, and only requires tactful experience of the real thing. Briefly, force retrieving consists of making a dog open its mouth and accept the carry, by putting pressure on ear, paw or lips. The object is slipped in and the pressure immediately ceased, thus creating an association of ideas in conjunction with an appropriate word of command. Once the dog will open its mouth, take and hold the dummy to order, the technique is gradually built up until it will find and retrieve the thrown and hidden dummy. Most certainly not an exercise to be inflicted upon a dog by a novice trainer.

SETTERS FOR ROUGHSHOOTING

I require an all-round working gundog for roughshooting, and am particularly attracted to setters, either English, Irish or Gordon. Are setters adaptable as maids-of-all-work, and which of the breeds would you recommend for the purpose?

Although some sportsmen have managed to train setters as all-rounders for roughshooting purposes, the breeds are not recommended, for several reasons. In the first place, they are not very fond of thick and thorny cover; their natural instinct is to range wide and far, and retrieving is not of much interest to them, so that forcing is usually necessary. Used for their traditional purpose – ranging large areas of open ground and setting game when winded – they are superb, and a joy to train and shoot over. If you particularly require a roughshooting dog which points as well as retrieving naturally and facing cover and water, then I would suggest that you consider one of the pointer-retriever breeds rather than an orthodox setter. It is worth remembering that both spaniels and retrievers can be taught to indicate the presence of game by standing or flash pointing, and that the most popular roughshooting dog is, undoubtedly, the English springer spaniel, due to its great versatility.

TRAINING EQUIPMENT

I am about to make my first attempt at gundog training, and have bought a Labrador and a springer, both aged six months and raring to go. Could you advise me what equipment I should invest in, and if there is any firm specializing in the manufacture of gundog training aids?

You will, obviously, require retrieving dummies, leads and,

possibly, a check cord. I also suggest that you invest in a dummy-launcher, a most versatile piece of equipment which can be used not only to accustom the pupils to gunfire and learn to mark and retrieve, but by intelligent use can be made to simulate ground game, towered birds and ducks skimming across water. All these items, and many others, are manufactured by Messrs Turner-Richards, Cardigan Street, Birmingham 4, who would be pleased to send you their brochures and price lists upon application.

GUNSHY OR GUN-NERVOUS?

My golden retriever, just a year old, is very put off by the sound of gunfire, even at a distance, and slinks back to heel, refusing to retrieve straight away and having to be patted and coaxed to do so. Do you consider that she is incurably gunshy, or should I persevere with her training?

The very fact that your bitch *will* retrieve within a minute or two of showing concern over gunfire encourages me to believe that she is not a hopeless case, and as she is so efficient in other directions I recommend that you give her more time. Try encouraging her by working with another dog, throwing a bird simultaneously with gunfire from a distance (jealousy may work), and also try getting someone to fire a shot while you are feeding her. In other words, do everything you can to associate her dread with something pleasant. Many of our most brilliant mature working gundogs have started off by being gun-nervous, but have been completely cured by perseverance, tact and ingenuity on the part of the handlers.

HUNTING COVER

What is the best method of getting a young dog hunting in thick cover? My retriever puppy does not seem at all keen to face anything tougher than rough grass, but will go like the clappers on a meadow and even in light roots. I want to use him as a quester for roughshooting, and so it is imperative that he will face thick hedges, bramble patches, etc.

I deprecate the use of retrievers as questers on roughshoots, because I consider that the orthodox questing breeds do the job so much better. However, having said that, any gundog worthy of the name should be capable of facing cover when necessary, even if only to retrieve therefrom. A puppy should be encouraged to regard cover as a natural environment from an early age, by tactful use of the dummy and by being taken for walks through stuff of increasing degrees of thickness. In the last resort, appeal can be made to his stomach by throwing titbits (meat, biscuits and the like) into cover, at first in sight of the dog and subsequently without his seeing you do so, and preferably when he is really hungry. You are thus associating cover with something very pleasant, and if in the course of his investigations the puppy comes across game or even game scent, the battle is half-won or may even be over! The example of a keen questing dog may work wonders in encouraging your puppy into the rough, but it is better to get him working solo; otherwise you may find that the youngster lets his schoolmaster do all the hunting and simply waits outside for him to put up something to chase, thus defeating the object and making the task of gaining steadiness all the more difficult.

PICKING UP AT SHOOTS

I am training a young golden retriever bitch for general purpose work – both rough and formal shooting – and she is nearly ready to take the field. I am wondering if, after a few days of shooting over her alone, it would be a good idea to take her picking up on a big shoot and, if so, how do I find a shoot willing to have us?

Picking up on a big shoot is probably the finest finishing school possible for a retriever, so long as you make absolutely certain that the dog is ready for field work, is not gun-nervous and is absolutely under command and unlikely to make a fool of you! As you will not be carrying a gun you can concentrate upon the dog, and try to keep that vital one jump ahead; with luck, you will also be able to choose your retrieves and give experience on different types of game and cover. Most big shoots welcome pickers-up with good dogs, and initial contact should be made to the host via his headkeeper. Indeed, the headkeeper is generally responsible for arranging for pickers-up as well as for beaters. If there are no keepered shoots in your vicinity about which you already know, I suggest you advertise or contact the secretary of your nearest field trial society, who may well be able to put you in touch with a keeper who would welcome your assistance on shooting days.

SPANIEL QUESTING

I am in the process of training my first English springer spaniel, and would like to know how far in front of me the dog should quest, and how I can teach correct ranging.

Ideally, a spaniel should quest up to twenty-five yards in front of, and to either side of, the handler/gun. If he ranges at greater distance, any game flushed is likely to be out-of-shot by the time the gun can be brought to bear on it. However, due allowance should always be made for wind direction, and a dog quartering downwind must, if it is to find game, range farther and work its ground back towards the handler. Something which many trainers, and even a few trial judges, seem apt to forget! Most well-bred working spaniels have a natural sense of range; this can be fostered and encouraged by tactful use of the stop and/or turn whistle and the appropriate hand signal, and also if the handler himself, *in the early stages*, weaves about and encourages his pupil to do likewise. This latter must be ceased as soon as the penny has dropped, because the whole object of spaniel work is for the gun to be able to maintain a comparatively straight course and get the dog to do the quartering. More specific instructions upon this question will be found in any good gundog training manual.

RETRIEVING THE REAL THING

My pointer puppy is showing great promise and is what I consider perfectly hand-trained, and now ready for more practical experience. However, he refuses to pick up the real thing (thrown or hidden), even though he delights in dummy work. How can I encourage him to lift fur and feather?

This not uncommon trouble is usually easily overcome by making the change-over from dummies to the real thing as natural and simple as possible. I suggest that you use freshly shot and clean *cold* game, encased in an old sock or stocking which should previously have been used as a dummy, thrown or hidden, stuffed with rags or wood wool, or even in the usual training dummy. This should, at first, be thrown a short distance into light cover; the dog should be sent for it quickly and the recall command or whistle given immediately, so as not to give the pupil too much time to stop, smell and think! If all goes well, repeat the process (running away and calling the dog urgently to speed him up if necessary) a couple of times. At the next session do exactly the same thing but with the game uncovered and in its natural state. Praise and pat the dog for good performance, and leave well alone until later the same day, or even the next day. Picking up the real thing is usually all a matter of confidence which, once instilled, is never lost. There are other ways and means of encouraging reluctant retrievers to carry game, including the use of another dog to arouse jealousy and a moderate course of so-called forcing. However, in the vast majority of cases the procedure I have outlined does the trick, and is much simpler for the average owner-trainer to carry out.

RETRIEVING SNIPE AND WOODCOCK

I am having difficulty with my Welsh springer over retrieving woodcock. Twice she has picked up the bird and started back towards me, only to drop it when about five yards away and roll on it, subsequently picking up again and delivering to hand. Have you any comments and suggestions?

Woodcock and snipe are notoriously unbeloved by retrieving dogs, and your experience is by no means uncommon. Whether it is the scent or the taste of the birds that puts dogs off, nobody knows, but given sufficient practice on these birds most dogs come to accept them and retrieve properly. Incidentally, I have frequently had the same experience with ducks when dogs were just commencing serious field work. The difficulty, of course, is to give sufficient experience on woodcock and snipe, because of their comparative scarcity on most shoots. However, I can confidently recommend a tip that the late Bill Brunt gave me years ago, and this is to practise dogs on dead starlings, using them as you would a dummy and, if necessary, first encasing them in a nylon stocking. I have invariably found that, once a dog will pick up and retrieve a starling happily, your worries are over.

HAVING A DOG PROFESSIONALLY TRAINED

I have been given a flat-coated retriever puppy of good working breeding, and am considering having him professionally trained. Would you advise me of the likely cost of this, at what age professionals like to start their pupils, and how long the training course would take?

Fees vary slightly from trainer to trainer, but the top men are now charging around £20–£25 per week (plus VAT). Most like the pupil to be between six and nine months of age when entering kennels, but this also varies and you should consult the man of your choice about it. Period of course varies according to (a) the ability of the dog, (b) the standard required and (c) luck! However, to train a retriever from scratch to a reasonably high standard usually takes from four to six months. The majority of established trainers find it difficult, if not impossible, to accept pupils at short notice, owing to the demand upon their services, and it is advisable to get your dog booked in as quickly as possible. All trainers require that pupils are vaccinated against the major canine diseases before entering their kennels, and emphasize that no guarantee can be given as to the success of the training course. I always advise that some form of written contract should be entered into between the parties concerned, so that both know just where they stand and what they are letting themselves in for!

DWELLING ON SCENTS WHEN AT HEEL

My golden retriever will persistently stop and dwell on scents when walking at heel, and I often find that she is several yards behind sniffing around or even breaking into hedges and starting to hunt. How can I break her of this annoying habit?

Hunting at heel is an aggravating fault in a gundog, and one which leads to major unsteadiness if not nipped in the bud very quickly. I suggest that you walk your bitch at heel where there is plenty of scent – for example along woodland rides – watching her like a hawk all the time; as soon as she puts her nose down on the scent give her a cut across the loins with a lead or switch, giving the ubiquitous command 'No!' in a very gruff voice at the same time. This is conditioning the reflexes at the psychological moment (in the actual commission of crime) and invariably has the desired effect. I only wish every fault in a gundog was as easy to correct!

RECALCITRANT SPANIEL

I own a springer spaniel one year old, which I wish to train to the gun. My problem is that when let off the lead she runs off and will not always return when called. I sent her away for training, but I had to get her back because the trainer could not do anything with her in the time required. How do I break this fault?

The short and simple answer is, 'Train her!' It seems to me that you are in too much of a hurry, and expected the trainer to whom you sent your bitch to work miracles in a very short time. Unless you have already taken her out shooting and allowed her to riot, or she is mentally unstable and completely unable to absorb education, it should be possible to inculcate obedience, even at the comparatively late age of a year. If you are not prepared to pay for her training by a professional, who would probably require four to six months in order to do the job properly, my advice is that you obtain a training manual and follow the instructions closely, and also to attend your nearest spaniel training classes.

The kingpin of obedience is sitting to command, which to begin with is taught while the pupil is on the lead, and subsequently when it is walking free. From here you build up to getting the dog to sit at a distance to command, signal and whistle; once you have reached this stage, getting it to return upon command should not be difficult. I am forwarding you a list of suitable books and the address of the secretary of your nearest spaniel training class. If it should be that you have already allowed the bitch to get on top of you and thoroughly out of hand, or if she is mentally unstable, then the only answer is to dispose of her and start afresh with another youngster of impeccable working breeding.

VALUE OF WORKING TESTS

Do you honestly *consider that gundog working tests are of real value to the shooting man training his own dog, or is your continual publicity of them motivated by commercialism or sympathy for a movement which, to me, seems determined to make tests a sport in their own right and is only interested in circus performances and the winning of trophies?*

Yes, I do honestly believe that working tests are of great practical value, not only to the gundog breeds but also to the shooting man. I was one of the pioneers of training classes and tests, for which I have no regrets – only great pride and gratification to have seen them catch on so well. While I fully appreciate that a minority of those participating may not be practical shooters but only trophy-hunters by and large the movement has done a very great deal for the breeds and for the education of the average owner-handler, and also a mammoth job in public relations for field sports. The list of handlers who have won top awards at field trials over the last twenty years, and who cut their teeth on gundog work at classes and tests, is a formidable one, and is proof of the pudding.

I do, however, entreat class and test fanatics to keep their priorities right and to remember that their functions are, or should be, a means to an end and not the end in themselves.

TEACHING TO JUMP

My Labrador puppy, now nine months old, seems reluctant to jump even the simplest obstacles and, as my shoot contains a lot of fences and gates, I am particularly anxious that he should be confident in this respect. I would appreciate your advice. He is basically a bold puppy and is starting to enter quite thick cover in search of the thrown dummy, but appears to have a mental block about fences!

Your puppy may have been put off negotiating obstacles, quite accidentally, in his early days, possibly through taking a nasty fall or becoming tangled up in a fence, perhaps even before you acquired him. This sort of experience leaves its mark and requires the restoration of confidence by very gentle and tactful means. Most Labradors are naturally bold jumpers and only require encouragement and experience to take bold, flying leaps over quite difficult obstacles. If you can find, or maybe construct, a low jump, preferably in a cul-de-sac, you may be able to entice him to negotiate it by use of the retrieving dummy, or even his bowl of food. If necessary, *help* him over the jump, crossing it yourself first of all, placing his paws on the top (which, naturally, should be solid), and enticing him either with food or by walking (or even running) away, calling and whistling him meanwhile. If success ensues, pat and praise him, and repeat the process a few times, and then gradually increase the height of the jump. As with swimming, once confidence is implanted, most dogs come to love the exercise and, henceforth, cannot get enough of it! The experience of another dog which is a bold jumper can also be invaluable, as dogs are great imitators, and a canine companion gives great confidence to a youngster.

RABBIT PEN

I am thinking of building a rabbit pen – a quarter of an acre in area – and seek your advice as to the best type of rabbit to put in it, and how many for a start?

My favourite type of rabbit for a pen of limited area is a Wild-Dutch cross in the first place but, as these are likely to be difficult, if not impossible, to obtain, I would suggest you start by stocking your pen with two or three pure-bred Dutch does (of any colour) and a healthy wild buck, and let nature take its course from there. If all goes well, within two or three generations you will find the inmates of wild colour (plus a white marking or two maybe), very active and prolific, not too keen on burrowing their way out. You will, however, have to restrict numbers and cull ruthlessly, otherwise your ground will not be able to support the population. In any event you will almost certainly have to provide clumps of artificial cover, and also to feed the stock well – I suggest rabbit pellets, wheat, roots and any greenfood. An adequate supply of water is also essential.

QUIVERING AT A DRIVE

My Labrador, which has just completed his first full season at driven game, shivers and quakes while waiting at a stand, although he never gives tongue or whines, and seldom moves. Various friends who have seen this seem to think that there must be something seriously wrong with him and that he ought not to be used at stud, which I am thinking of doing as he is such a good worker. What say you?

With friends like yours, who needs enemies! I suspect that they are suffering from a dose of sour grapes and are jealous of your dog's working ability. The symptoms he develops at a stand are nothing more than sheer excitement and tension – eagerness to get on with the job if you like – and you should count your blessings that this does not manifest itself in whining or restlessness, which really are serious faults. Lots of dogs act just as you describe when raring to go, especially in their first season or two, and I do not think for one moment that you have anything to worry about or need have the slightest qualms about breeding from him.

CHOKE CHAINS

My golden retriever is very boisterous and disobedient, and I have been advised to use a choke chain and lead in training. However, my wife feels that choke chains are cruel and too hard on the dog. Can you suggest an effective alternative?

I have no hesitation whatsoever in using a choke chain on a powerful and boisterous dog which quickly learns good manners if the chain is properly applied. Dogs have very tough necks, and the discomfort created by sharp jerks and the tightening of the chain is of short duration but very effective, and really the only way thoroughly to discipline a strong dog. An alternative is the nylon (cord or webbing) or harness leather choke lead, which the majority of trainers use as standard on all but their most difficult pupils; these are certainly milder in their effect on the pupil, however hard they are jerked. However, as your dog sounds to be something of a hard case, I advocate using the choke *chain* until you have made him see the error of his ways, after which you could utilize a choker of softer material.

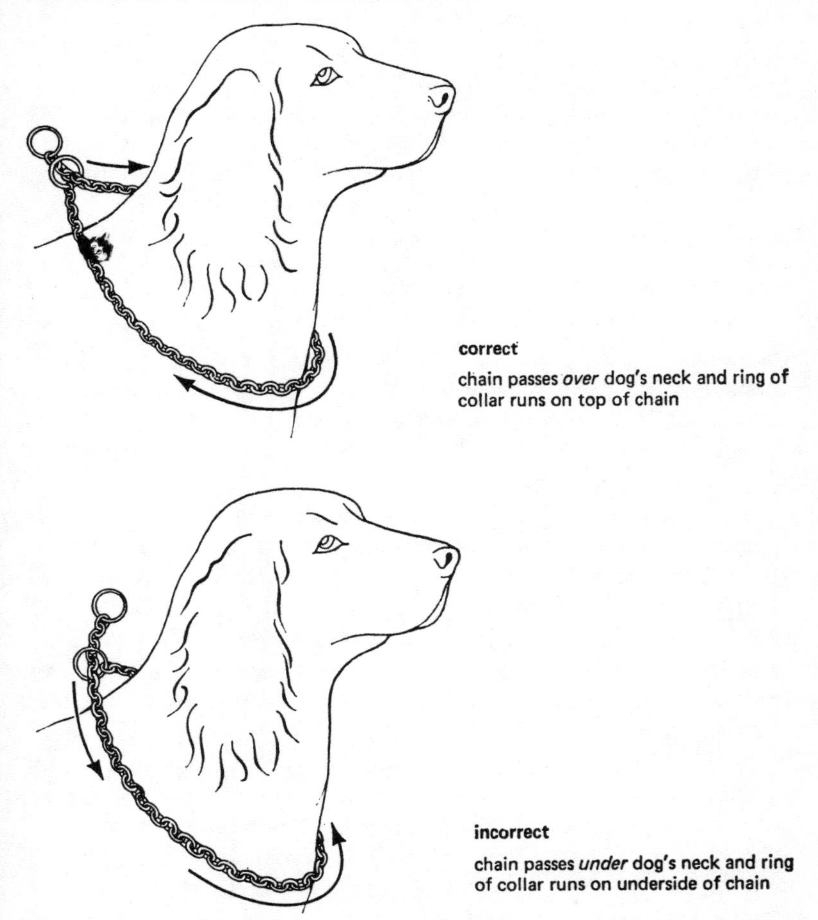

Correct and incorrect methods of using the choke chain or lead. These diagrams assume that the dog is being worked on the handler's left-hand side.

WHINING AT DRIVES

My husband has taken our Labrador puppy, aged ten months, to shoots on three occasions to enable her to experience the real thing, after training her at home to heel, sit, stay and retrieve, all of which she does beautifully. On the shoots, however, she whined incessantly, became extremely excited, and played deaf when more than ten yards away. On finding a bird, she retrieved perfectly, only to start whining until the next time. What can we do?

This sounds like a typical example of being in too much of a hurry in training. At ten months of age your puppy should only really be *starting* her education. Whining is symptomatic both of excitability and insufficient training, and I fear that it is now too late to do anything about it. Punishment will probably only make matters worse. Nobody has yet come up with the cure for whining, which is, rightly an eliminating fault at field trials and an aggravating (and catching) nuisance on a shoot. Whining is often a hereditary fault, and you may have a puppy of the wrong breeding anyway, even though you have obviously rushed things. Start again with another puppy, and benefit from your mistakes.

RELUCTANCE TO RETRIEVE

My Welsh springer is a grand hunter, and even won a prize at a test for the best quester, but prefers questing to retrieving when there is attractive scent about. At home he retrieves the dummy perfectly and gives no worries. What can I do to get him retrieving in the field?

Welsh springers, unfortunately, are notorious for the very fault that you have described, which undoubtedly, is one reason why they are not more popular and we do not see them competing in any field trial stakes. They have wonderful noses and are quite fearless in cover, but the majority want to get on with the questing and to hell with picking up and retrieving, although, to be fair, there are quite a few exceptions about which retrieve very willingly and naturally.

Much as I dislike and deprecate the practice, the only answer in these cases of dogs which retrieve only when they feel like it is a thorough course of force retrieving. This is a very time-consuming and backbreaking procedure for the handler and, in my opinion, no job for the novice owner-trainer, because it is so easy to make matters worse rather than better unless you know what you are about. There are various professional trainers who will undertake the job, though none, of course, will guarantee success, nor will they tie themselves down to time.

REGISTERING A DOG WITHOUT PAPERS

I have a two-year-old springer bitch but, unfortunately, I did not collect the pedigree papers from the breeder, who has since left the area. I wondered whether you could advise me if it is possible to register her with the Kennel Club on her own merit, and if so what I must do. I have access to the sire's pedigree if that will help.

Yours is a very common story, and I am constantly emphasizing in my articles the desirability of obtaining the necessary documents with any dog that is bought. The Kennel Club will only accept for registration a dog which has both parents registered, with the names and registered numbers entered on Form 1A, and the signature of the breeder. If the breeder's signature is unobtainable, a good reason for this must be supplied. It therefore appears unlikely that you will be able to register your bitch, unless you can obtain the essential registration names and numbers of the parents, and offer convincing proof of your inability to obtain the signature of the breeder. The address of the Kennel Club is 1 Clarges Street, London W1A 8AB, and I suggest that you write to the secretary and put your case before him.

BREEDING

I am contemplating breeding from my English springer bitch, now aged nine months and just starting her first season. Is this too early to mate her? Also, I would like to know how I go about selecting a suitable stud dog, and the time when the bitch is likely to be most receptive to the dog.

It is not advisable to breed from a bitch as early as nine months, and you would be best advised to wait until she has her second heat, by which time she should be fully mature, physically and mentally. As regards the selection of a suitable mate for her, this will depend upon her breeding and how much you are prepared to spend upon the stud fee. It is quite a good idea to consult the breeder of the bitch, who, after all, has a vested interest in the matter and, if experienced and reputable, can be relied upon to put you on the right lines. The optimum time to send a bitch to the stud dog is between the tenth and fourteenth day of oestrum and, wherever possible, I recommend that she be given two services with a day in between. This may entail leaving her at the kennels for a few days, but is well worth while and, usually, the stud fee charged includes her keep for a reasonable period.

VACCINATIONS AND BOOSTERS

We are shortly acquiring a Vizla puppy to be trained for the gun, and would like to know what vaccinations against disease you recommend, and at what age they should be given. Is it necessary to have booster injections from time to time or, as we live in the heart of the country, would these be a waste of money?

Every puppy should be vaccinated against the major canine diseases at as early an age as possible, as recommended by your veterinary surgeon, usually between eight and twelve weeks. A course of two injections, given at fourteen-day intervals, will cover the dog against canine parvovirus, distemper, hardpad, leptospiral jaundice and virus hepatitis. Booster doses are recommended every one or two years, and here again your vet will advise you. A country-dwelling dog is probably even more susceptible to these diseases then one which lives in a town, as it is more liable to come into contact with rats, and also has less opportunity for building up a natural immunity. Vaccination is a wonderful insurance, and if you value your dog you will not begrudge the cost, which is around £25 for the initial course and £10 to £12 for boosters.

COAT CASTING

Our yellow Labrador, aged eighteen months, is continually casting his coat, and has done so since puppyhood. My wife, who is somewhat house-proud, is becoming exasperated, and even threatening that either we get rid of the dog or she will leave home! As he is a very good worker, and of delightful temperament with the children, it would break our hearts to part with him. Have you any suggestions about controlling continual moult?

Excessive coat-shedding is a common complaint against yellow Labradors, especially those which live indoors! Yellows certainly do appear to be looser-coated than blacks, but this may well be because the hairs are more obvious on carpets and furnishing. Regular grooming with a suitable brush (I recommend a short-bristled stiff, or even wire, brush) can prove helpful, but the remedy that I, and countless owners to whom I have recommended it, have found most effect is to give the dog a walnut-sized lump of margarine (*not* butter) every day. This will be eaten with relish, either on its own or mixed in the usual diet. Why it works I do not know, but it may be due to the vitamin A and D content of margarine, which is easily assimilated. I even know of several veterinary surgeons who recommend the margarine trick, and it is not uncommon for owners of yellow Labradors to bring along a tub of margarine for me to give their dogs while they are in kennels for boarding.

CONTROLLING SKIN VERMIN

Every spring and summer my dogs become infested with both fleas and lice, which I have difficulty in ridding them of. We use straw for bedding in the kennels, both winter and summer, and once a week swill down the kennels and runs with disinfectant. Ought we to cut out using straw, and can you recommend any powder or spray which we can use to control this infestation?

I must confess to being a straw hater! I have invariably found that this encourages skin vermin, especially during warm weather, and that it does little or nothing for the comfort of the kennel inmates. My own dogs sleep on bare boards, winter and summer, without any ill-effects, and I experience very little trouble with fleas or lice among them. Providing that your other hygiene precautions are adequate, I suggest that you make a regular practice of dusting both the dogs and their kennel benches with a powder containing benzine hexachloride dust (Gamma B.H.C.), obtainable from veterinary surgeons or veterinary chemists, every week or ten days. There are also various aerosol sprays which can be used on the dogs, to kill and inhibit fleas and lice, one of the most effective being 'Nuvan Top', manufactured by Ciba-geigy (UK) Ltd, Whittlesford, Cambridge CB2 4QT. This is quite safe if used according to directions, and prevents re-infestation for up to two weeks.

KENNELS FOR GUNDOGS

I have kept gundogs for many years, but only one at a time and always in the house. I am shortly retiring and intend taking up breeding a few Labradors and springers as a hobby, and perhaps training one or two for other people. Obviously I shall require kennels, especially as I have no outbuildings which can be adapted, even though I have a couple of acres of garden. I do not wish to go to the expense of building anything too permanent, in case we move, so I assume that portable, sectional wooden kennels are my best bet. Can you give me the addresses of any specialists in this field, including that of a firm which might be prepared to build to my own specifications?

Good kennelling is absolutely essential if you intend setting up a breeding-training establishment, and while wooden buildings have their disadvantages (including the ease with which dogs can and will chew them unless they are appropriately protected with metal on accessible projections!) they are comfortable, warm, easily repaired and, above all, portable. Many of the older hands in the dog business much prefer wooden kennels for these reasons. There are several firms specializing in sectional kennelling, and I suggest that you contact Messrs A. Neaverson & Sons Ltd, Peakirk, near Peterborough (telephone [0733] 252225), specifying your requirements and asking for brochures and quotations.

WORMING PUPPIES AND ADULT DOGS

Our golden retriever bitch has just whelped a splendid litter of seven pups, and we are wondering at what age they should be wormed and which vermifuge you recommend. Should the bitch also be wormed, and do you believe in regular worming of pups and adults, even if no worms are seen in their stools?

Young puppies almost inevitably develop roundworms which, if not treated will retard their growth and create all sorts of problems. Modern vermifuges are both safe and effective, and can be obtained either through a veterinary chemist or from your vet. I strongly recommend consulting the latter. The earliest age at which pups should be wormed is between four and six weeks, according to the drug used, and dosage is usually by weight. Adult dogs and puppies should, in my opinion, be wormed as a routine every few months; adults are most likely to harbour tapeworm (plus, perhaps, a few roundworms), no matter how well they are fed and managed. I will not stick my neck out by recommending any particular product, but simply repeat that your veterinary surgeon is the best man to consult on this important subject.

VICIOUS SPANIEL

Our eight-year-old springer spaniel bitch has recently developed a very uncertain temper, especially towards children; she has now bitten (for no apparent reason) our own boy twice and a friend's daughter once, and, on rare occasions, shows an aggressive attitude towards my wife and even myself. The bitch seems fit and healthy and, as far as I am aware, has never been teased by the children or ill-treated by anyone. Can you suggest a remedy, or ought we to have her put down?

Without first-hand knowledge of the bitch, it is difficult to suggest a cure, even if there is one, for this worrying problem. For myself, I will not tolerate a dog of unreliable temperament no matter how good a worker it may be, especially if there are young children in the family. It is bad enough if the dog bites one of your own children, but far worse if it attacks an outsider, which might well involve you in expensive litigation, quite apart from the humanitarian aspect. So, drastic though it may seem, my advice is to have the bitch put down as soon as possible. I would like to emphasize here that this nasty streak which your springer has developed is quite out of character for the breed, and may be regarded as the exception which proves the rule.

MILK OR WATER?

Our five-year-old pointer puppy hardly ever seems to drink water, but will take all the milk we offer her. Is this unusual, and should we harden our hearts and cease giving her milk in an effort to make her accept water as a cheaper substitute?

All the time you take the line of least resistance and use milk, the puppy will, very naturally, look for it and prefer it to plain water. However, milk (while being a very complete and nourishing drink-cum-feed) is not strictly necessary for a puppy of five months, and I think you should phase it out, unless you wish to make a rod for your own back. I am quite certain that if there is always a bowl of water available to your pointer, she will drink it when she is thirsty enough, and be all the better for it. Almost any dog will drink milk, thirsty or not, if offered it, but will only take water when it is really necessary.

ONE MEAL OR TWO

I have a golden retriever and a G.S.P., both over one year old, and, up to now, have been feeding them only one meal per day. However, my wife thinks that they should have two feeds and we have decided to ask you to arbitrate for us! We are feeding on one of the complete, all-in pelleted diets that you recommend but the dogs always seem hungry, even though they are in good condition.

Traditionally, adult dogs are fed once a day, but experience has taught me that the majority of dogs (especially if kept in kennels) do far better on two meals, all the more so if receiving the balanced, all-in food. I normally feed my own dogs one third of the daily total in the morning, and the balance in the evening. This seems to keep them more contented throughout the day, and prevents them gorging themselves too much. Incidentally, I have found that pelleted food is best fed scattered and not in a bowl, as greedy dogs are liable almost to choke themselves by gobbling it up too fast – which is another recommendation for twice-daily feeding. Remember that, when feeding dry foods, drinking water must always be available to the dogs.

DEPRAVED HABIT

My Weimaraner puppy has the disgusting habit of eating its faeces in the kennel run, and no amount of punishment seems to have any effect. What is the reason for this trouble, and how can I cure it?

This is a not uncommon problem among dogs housed in kennels, both puppies and adults. The cause varies, and may be due to worm infestation, lack of vitamins and/or minerals, sheer boredom, or a combination of all three. I suggest, therefore, that you dose you puppy for worms (preferably obtaining advice and the necessary tablets from your veterinary surgeon), make certain that you are feeding it on a sensible diet containing adequate vitamins and minerals, and reduce the length of time it is incarcerated in the kennel run. Exercise it outside as often as possible and certainly immediately after meals, if this can be arranged.

DIETARY SUPPLEMENT

We are contemplating breeding from our Irish water spaniel bitch this year, and wonder what, if any, alteration should be made to her diet during pregnancy, and if you would recommend a vitamin-mineral supplement to give her, both before and after whelping?

So long as your bitch is receiving an adequate diet, no alteration need be made during the first few weeks of pregnancy, but when she becomes heavy in whelp I suggest you give her two or three smaller meals each day instead of one large one, to avoid discomfort. I can thoroughly recommend Canovel as a supplement during both pregnancy and lactation. This is manufactured by

Messrs Beecham Animal Health, Great West Road, Brentford. Middlesex, and is available from veterinary surgeons and chemists.

RAT PROBLEM

I am having trouble with rats around the kennels. We do not appear to have many, but they are doing a lot of burrowing and I have seen them in the sleeping quarters with the dogs. The traps I have set have not proved effective, but I am loath to use poison because of the danger to the dogs. Have you any practical suggestions to make?

Rats around the kennels are a real menace, and you should deal with the infestation before it becomes too serious. For several years now I have been successful in keeping the rat population round my kennels at virtually nil by the use of Townex rat poison, which comes in small plastic sachets, virtually weatherproof, that can be put down the rat holes or (under cover) along the runs. Naturally you must guard against the dogs (or, for that matter, children) having access to the poison, and also burn or bury any rodent bodies which you pick up. This presentation of rat poison in sachets is speedy, effective, ideal for kennel and stable use, and as near foolproof as possible, if the baiting instructions are carefully followed.

CANKER REMEDY

My spaniel is suffering from ear canker, which my vet has been unable to cure, despite trying various remedies. I wonder if you would let me have the formula of the old fashioned powder which Dick Sharpe used to use and recommend with such success during the twenties?

The Dick Sharpe canker remedy is still quite widely used in gundog kennels, and often proves effective where other treatments have failed but chronic canker of long standing may require surgery, especially in elderly dogs. However, in the case of your dog it is well worth trying. The formula, which can be made up by any chemist, is: 1 oz. boracic powder, 1 oz. zinc powder and 1 dram iodoform, well mixed. Dust this into the ears, after cleaning them with a cotton-wool swab, once or twice a day.

BASKET OR BOX?

We are shortly acquiring a gundog puppy which, for the time being at any rate, will have to live in the house. Do you recommend that it should be given a box or a basket to sleep in, and in which room should it be kept?

Dog baskets are an abomination, in my opinion, and I would go for a strong wooden box (preferably with metal round the edges to inhibit chewing), which should be placed in whichever room is most convenient for you and least likely to be damaged by the inevitable early accidents and the puppy's natural destructiveness! If you have an enclosed verandah, lobby or storeroom with a minimum of contents at tooth-level, so much the better. If you intend ultimately to keep the pup in an outside kennel, you certainly do not want to start it off in the kitchen!

SARCOPTIC MANGE

I have a seven-month-old dog which has been diagnosed as suffering from sarcoptic mange, but the treatment given to date has not proved effective. Can you suggest a reliable remedy?

The only certain way of diagnosing the two forms of mange (sarcoptic and follicular) is by examination of a skin scraping under the microscope, and I assume that this has been done in the case of your dog. Sarcoptic mange is comparatively easy to cure, one of the most effective dressings being Coopers Mange Dressing (Skin Dressing No. 3), which is manufactured by Messrs Cooper, McDougall & Robertson Ltd, Berkhamsted, Hertfordshire, and is obtainable from veterinary chemists. Two or three baths in the solution, prepared according to the manufacturer's instructions, at seven- to fourteen-day intervals, should effect a complete cure. I stress, however, that the dog can re-infect itself unless bedding, kennel, etc., are thoroughly disinfected at the time of the first treatment. Follicular mange, on the other hand, is extremely stubborn and often incurable, and is believed to be hereditary. A drug called Hexon–20 and various dressings, which can only be obtained through veterinary surgeons, who should always be consulted in doubtful cases, are occasionally successful.

SPAYING

I have recently acquired a golden retriever bitch puppy and, as we live in a big village with a large dog population, am considering the advisability of having her spayed, for obvious reasons. Do you approve of this and, if so, at what age should the operation be performed, and is it likely to have any ill effects upon her working ability?

While I am, generally speaking, against interference with nature, I can appreciate your problem (which is not uncommon!), but suggest that you think seriously before taking the drastic step of having your bitch spayed. If you have a good kennel and run for her, wherein she can be enclosed when in season, or, alternatively, are prepared to put her in boarding kennels during the periods of oestrum, then I should definitely advise against the operation, not only because I have found so many owners regretting being unable to breed from a good working bitch later in her life, but also because of the tendency for spayed bitches to put on excessive weight and become lethargic, requiring vigilant attention to diet. In *some* instances spaying seems to have a deleterious effect upon training and working ability, and the temperament, but nothing like as much as does the castrating of a dog. If you decide to go ahead with the project, your veterinary surgeon will advise you of the optimum time to have the operation performed, which is usually after the first period of oestrum or, probably better still, after the bitch has been allowed to breed one litter. In my limited experience of spaying, the later the operation, the less effect it is likely to have upon the bitch's performance in the field and general temperament.

YELLOW LABRADORS

Am I right in stating that all Labradors are called 'yellow' if they are any shade of colour from red to silver? Also, someone told me that yellow Labradors are more difficult to train and more boisterous than blacks. Is there any truth in this statement?

People often refer to yellow Labradors as 'golden', but this is quite incorrect and officially, from the Kennel Club's point of view, the classification is definitely 'yellow', no matter if the shade is fox-red or cream. There are, of course, black Labradors, and also that rare but attractive colour, chocolate.

In my experience, yellow Labradors (or, for that matter, chocolates) are not more difficult to train, or more boisterous, than blacks. However, I have found that, generally speaking, yellows do not seem as bold in cover as blacks or chocolates, and some breeders consider them more delicate, healthwise, though this may be pure imagination! For the record, the best cover Labrador I ever trained was yellow, and a keeper friend of mine had a chocolate from me which ought to have been a spaniel, so forcefully did he thrash thick and thorny cover. Which seems to prove that one should not generalize!

'GOLDEN' LABRADORS OF DIFFERENT SHADES

I have just bred a litter of golden Labrador pups from my bitch, sired by a golden dog of the same dark shade, and am horrified to discover that the colour of the pups varies considerably, some being almost white. Has something gone wrong?

The only thing that has gone wrong appears to be your knowledge of Labradors and canine genetics! In the first place, there is no such thing as a 'golden' Labrador. The breed standard lays down that the colour is black, chocolate or *yellow* – which may be from fox-red to cream – free from any white markings. The coat should be whole-coloured and not of flecked appearance, but a small white spot on the chest is allowable. You should be careful to refer to your 'golden' Labradors as 'yellow', thus avoiding confusion with the entirely separate and different breed, golden retrievers. Litters of yellow Labradors, even from parents of identical shade, almost always vary in colouration and, indeed, you can even get blacks and/or chocolates among them. Yellows and chocolates evolved as sports from the original blacks, and cannot be relied upon to breed true to colour and shade. A very valuable book for you would be *All about the Labrador*, by Mary Roslin-Williams (Pelham Books £4.25), which deals very thoroughly with the breed in all its aspects, and gives a very concise treatise on breeding and genetics.

DOCKING SPANIEL PUPPIES

Our springer bitch is expecting a litter of pups shortly, and I would be glad to have your comments on docking. I believe pups intended for work usually have longer tails than show dogs, so I would like to know how much tail to remove.

Any form of docking is considered by some to be a mutilation, but practical working spaniel men consider the operation essential for several reasons; however, they always insist that the dog is left with plenty of flag to wave (which show-docked dogs do not have!), as half the joy of watching a spaniel at work is provided by the happy and stylish tail action, which a show stump cannot possibly display. When docking my own puppies, I remove just over one third of the tail, and always endeavour to leave a white tip if this is possible. As a rough guide, stretch out a hind leg of the pup and pull the tail down along it, snipping off the length that extends beyond the patella joint.

UNDERSHOT PUPPY

I have just taken delivery of a golden retriever puppy, and am horrified to discover that it is terribly undershot, which is not only unsightly but will, I am told, affect his work. Is this a serious fault, and can anything be done to correct it?

As you say, an undershot (some people call it 'pig-jawed') dog is unsightly, and it certainly is a fault, usually hereditary, so far as the show ring is concerned. However, if the dog is only required for work, I do not think you need worry unduly. I have trained several undershot youngsters, and none of them had the slightest difficulty in picking up and carrying game, although some of my professional colleagues have had contrary experiences. As far as I know, nothing can be done, surgically or otherwise, to correct this deformity of the jaw, and, in the interests of the breed, the dog should most certainly not be used at stud.

BONES

I have been told never, on any account, to give my retriever puppy bones to chew, not only because this might make her hard-mouthed, but because it is also dangerous, and detrimental to her teeth. What is your opinion?

I believe the advice you have been given is totally wrong, and in over thirty years of running a gundog kennels I have never found bones – *which must be raw and large* – detrimental in any way. In fact, for several years during and just after the last war, I fed split, raw sheeps' heads to my dogs, without any ill effects either upon their mouths or their health generally. Bones of the correct type, given once or twice a week, are beneficial, and help to keep the teeth clean and tartar-free and, in the case of a young puppy, reduce the possibilities of damage to furniture and/or kennels! After all, the dog is a carnivorous animal which, in the wild state, would be dealing with raw bones as a matter of course. But never, on any account, feed cooked bones of any description, nor poultry, rabbit or game bones, unless fully processed in a pressure cooker.

7

Refinements and summary of training

REFINEMENTS OF EDUCATION

There are a few refinements which can be imparted to the education of any dog, and which will not only prove useful but will bring a glow of pride into the proud handler's face when he shows off these qualities before his admiring friends. I have not touched upon them before for the simple reason that they should only be taught if the trainer has ample time, patience and opportunity, and because I wished the essential accomplishments to be stressed first and foremost.

What are these refinements? Pointing is one, and I have dealt fairly fully with this. Introduce your dog to game when he is wearing a check cord, and when it is obvious that he has spotted something, take hold of the end and prevent him from flushing until you give the order, when he should immediately be made to drop. The success or otherwise of this lesson depends upon the dog's natural instincts, but practically any dog can thus be encouraged to give the shooter warning of the presence of game.

Sitting to the stamp of the foot is another very useful accomplishment, and can also be taught fairly easily. By regularly stamping one foot when giving the signal to sit most dogs will ultimately learn to sit to the stamp alone, and when out shooting it often occurs that one has no free hand with which to signal and the use of the voice is undesirable. I should imagine that when ferreting rabbits, for instance, or indeed when shooting rabbits sitting out, this signal would be useless and defeat its own ends, as a stamp is the rabbits' warning of danger. For ordinary game shooting the stamp of the foot will not cause much disturbance however.

I have previously mentioned making a dog sit before being allowed to touch his food, and besides being a very useful item of discipline and teaching patience at the drop, I consider this a very desirable refinement of training, because the dog gets into the habit of refusing to touch food unless he receives the order from his handler, and in these days of indiscriminate poison-laying for vermin this may save the life of your dog. I have a springer bitch who, although she will sit before eating her food, is not above picking up any bones that she may find lying about, but will always bring them to me before eating them, presumably for my inspection and approval. If they should be rabbit or poultry bones, which she knows full well are forbidden, she approaches me with a very guilty look in her eyes, and willingly surrenders them, quite resigned to the fact that they will be put out to salvage on the morrow!

We now come to that very vexed question of a dog working the opposite side of a hedge to his master. Some are for this idea, and others very much against, but I suppose that this can be called a refinement, and as such is worthy of inclusion under that heading. I think whether this is an advantage or not depends a great deal upon the type of shoot, and the reliability of the dog, but suffice to say that if you wish a dog to do this work he should not be allowed on the other side of a hedge until he is reliable under your eyes. When worked in this manner the handler should not stand immediately opposite his dog, but at an angle and some way out from the hedge. Many dogs will take to doing this naturally, and any dog which learns for himself that the gun is the most reliable method of bagging game will often take to heading off a rabbit or pheasant, and so flushing it in the direction of the shooter. Personally, I like to see my dogs at work, and unless I am convinced that working my dog on the opposite side of a particular hedge is the very best way to secure a shot, I prefer to have them working on the same side as myself.

SUMMARY

By way of summarizing what I have already written about the training of an all-round gundog for the roughshooter, it might be a good idea for me to stress the main points that should be borne in mind. I have stated before that no dog should be trained by hard and fast rules, because of the variations in canine mentality, but the chief rules by which the trainer should guide his pupil in the way he should go can be given, and any puzzles that crop up during the training can, as a rule, be solved by the application of common sense and, what is even more important, by regarding them from the dog's point of view.

In the first place, I have recommended the roughshooter to invest (and I use the word invest intentionally) in an English springer spaniel, of working strain. While not condemning those who use a retriever of any breed for this work, I have found from long experience of all breeds that the springer will adapt himself better to the various duties expected of the dog of all work, besides which he has that drive which is so essential to the hunter-up of game. When I say that my heart sinks when I am sent a retriever to be trained as an all-rounder, you will understand that I know full well that I am in for a much harder job of work than had the aspirant been a springer. The show bench and the popularity of cockers as ladies' pets (how I detest those obese creatures one sees dragging their mistresses along on a lead!) have done a lot to create distrust of spaniels generally by the unknowledgeable sportsman, but most strains of springer retain their working qualities, and those bred from workers by gamekeepers and sportsmen are not to be confounded with the delicate and hysterical creatures to which I allude above. Enough said.

An unspoiled puppy is essential for successful training, and the earlier the obedience lessons are started, providing they are not overdone, the better. Retrieving, too, can be encouraged from a tender age, care being taken not to sicken the puppy of this, and never to pull anything from his mouth, but to encourage a willing delivery. The crux of the training is the drop and a puppy which will drop to command and signal, and walk to heel obediently, can safely be taken anywhere, and will be easy to handle when it comes to field work.

As soon as the early lessons, sit, heel, retrieving and obedience to call, are thoroughly mastered, the puppy should be gradually introduced to the gun. Firing a rifle or small bore at ever-diminishing distances during mealtimes is a good way of accustoming the youngster to noise, and the lesson can be utilized from the first to make the pupil drop to shot. This is easy and obvious if you do as I recommend: always make your pupil sit and await the word of command before touching his food. The excitement of seeing his meal in front of him will diminish his fear of the report, and gradually he will connect the three acts, shooting, sitting and eating. Thereafter the noise of a gun will link up in his mind with something pleasant.

I devoted a whole article to the subject of punishment, and at the time stated that more failures were produced by lack of understanding and punishing either unjustly or not at all than from any other cause. A great deal of well-intentioned nonsense has been written upon this subject by people who should know better, and the old school of brute force and ignorance is giving way to almost namby-pamby methods of training, which are nearly as bad! Punishment is certainly better dispensed with if possible, but most dogs at some time or another commit a fault which, if allowed to pass unchastised, will be repeated over and over again, and ultimately become incurable. Far better, therefore, to make sure that the pupil knows what he has done wrong upon the first occasion, and thereafter punish him sufficiently to deter him on future occasions. The whole art of punishing a dog is to keep your temper, to make him realize that you intend to maintain discipline, and, most important of all, to be sure that he knows the why and wherefore of the chastisement. Immediately after the offence is the time, and the scene of the crime is the place for the whipping, which should most certainly not be more severe than is essential, with due regard to your dog's nature. No dog should ever be cowed or made jumpy by punishment, but if common sense is used this advice should be quite superfluous. A dog which has received just (note the word just) punishment will hold his master in far higher esteem than the animal who thinks he has bested his handler and got away with it. A dog's psychology in this respect is very akin to that of the human. Punish him with something soft, such as a lead, and never strike your puppy over the head, or use your feet upon him.

Another important point to be considered is the environment of your puppy. I have said that, if possible, your dog should live in, and see as much of you as he can, always providing that discipline is maintained and that liberties are not allowed. If, however, you are away a lot or there is a danger of the puppy being spoiled by the good intentions of the family, he should spend his off-duty hours in a kennel, not chained to a barrel, but in a properly constructed house with a small run, a converted outhouse or disused garage. Providing the place is draught- and waterproof and that you supply a raised bench for him to sleep on your dog will probably be happier here than roaming about masterless all day doing untold damage to his training.

I crave forgiveness if, in this summary, I mention anything that I have not said before, but in dog training new features are always cropping up, and it is my wish to impart as much knowledge to the tyro as is possible in the space at my disposal.

No puppy should be taken into the field until he has learned the early obedience lessons, will retrieve the dummy well up to hand, and has perhaps been allowed to carry the real thing and have one or two of the invaluable scent-trail lessons.

The main thing, with a general-purpose dog, is to instil a love of hunting, be it for wounded or unwounded game, and no gun should be carried at first. Prior to this, the puppy should have been encouraged to jump fences and other obstacles, and enter water willingly. At first, quarter the ground as you will wish your pupil to do, and try to persuade him to hunt. Only give short lessons, never tire or bore him, and do not force the pup into thick cover. When he comes upon game, let him flush it and then drop him, and in the case of rabbits never let him follow up the line. Practise him to turn to a whistle and to obey hand signals, and keep him within a twenty-five-yard radius.

When he is steady to game and rabbits, take the pupil out at heel and fire blanks at the birds or rabbits that you put up; thereafter, if he has remained steady, allow him out to hunt and follow the same procedure. Do not give him a retrieve under natural conditions until you are assured of his steadiness, and then only send him out for game which has fallen out of sight, and which is quite dead and free from blood. When he picks up, walk away quickly, and take the game from him on the move.

The retrieving of runners is only undertaken when your pup has gained experience with stone-dead game, and do not be disappointed at initial failures. Experience will put all these little things right. I strongly recommend every type of dog to be used as a no-slip retriever during the early part of his first proper season. Minor acts of disobedience can thereby be readily corrected.

The check cord should be carried during all these early field

The shotgun should be introduced very tactfully . . .

. . . and not be fired over the dog until confidence has been instilled

Directing the pupil out to the retrieve by clear hand signal

Hunting along a hedge.

Above: The dog has winded game, draws up to it . . .

. . . and enthusiastically investigates the hedge to flush

Water practice

Above: The specially constructed canvas dummy . . .

. . and a gently shelving pool are ideal

Water practice

Above: An experienced, water-loving companion is a great help in giving a youngster confidence. Let them play about together in the shallows for a start, preferably on a warm day

Mission accomplished!

work operations, and used in the case of wilful disobedience or unsteadiness. Do not, in your effort to obtain steadiness, cow the pup – rather, judge his temperament and, if he is inclined to be slow, allow licence. If he is of a headstrong disposition, keep him on the early work longer and correct faults immediately. Avoid taking the pup out with other dogs, unless he is dead steady, and give the cold shoulder to any shooting companion who is likely to interfere, intentionally or otherwise, with the working of your dog. Finally, give your dog as much work as you possibly can, but not long spells at a time. Do not go shooting with a large party until you are sure of your dog's behaviour, and at all times *try to see the dog's point of view*!

That, I think, is a quick and fair summary of all that I have so far written on the subject. There are, of course, many different methods of training a gundog, each of which has its adherents, but after training one or two dogs most men produce one or two little tricks of their own, and I confess to having, in my early days of training, read every available book on the subject, and then proceeded to train on the various systems. My final system of training is accordingly based upon the most useful items gleaned from these books, plus innumerable points learned from actual experience with different breeds. As with the dog, so with the trainer – experience of a practical kind will produce the results.

It is my opinion that the man who keeps one, or at the most two, really well-trained gundogs for general work will enjoy the happiest results and the best days abroad with his gun. On a small shoot, the dog of the one-dog man gets to know the lie of the land better than his master, with the result that he does his work in a truly brilliant manner. On the other hand, the owner of several dogs is often in a quandary as to which dog to take out. If he takes them all out, they run wild; if he takes the same one time and again, the others get neglected; and if he gives each a turn (unless he does a vast amount of shooting) not one ever becomes really good. Unless you are a breeder or trainer, or both, or have an exceptionally large shoot, I consider it criminal folly in these days to keep more than one gundog when it is possible to train a single animal to do the work of several. General Hutchinson, way back in 1848, said that he did not consider a 'regular land retriever' to be worth its keep if a pointer or setter could be trained to retrieve. Today, I say the same about them, providing that you own a good spaniel.

It has been impossible in the course of this book to say all that could be said on the subject of training a gundog, and even given the space I do not pretend that I could say enough! I sincerely hope that I have not trodden on too many corns, and if I have made any glaring omissions I will do my best to rectify them on a future occasion. My readers have been very generous with pen and ink, and have given me much food for thought and many valuable tips, which will be passed on, in due course, to others as greedy as myself for information concerning the welfare of the gundog breeds.

My best thanks are due to all interested readers and correspondents, and I offer my apologies to those whose ideas upon this vast subject do not coincide with mine. What I have written has been a genuine attempt to assist the novice to obtain the best from a puppy of gundog breed, founded upon my past experiences. If, as a result of much burning of midnight oil and writer's cramp, I have assisted but one spaniel to find and retrieve his rabbit more speedily, or have prevented the unjust chastisement of one retriever for a fault which was not his but his master's then I have succeeded in my mission, and the enjoyment I have received from writing this book is made complete.

8

The trained dog and the slack hunter

BUYING A TRAINED DOG

One of the worst jobs on earth for the experienced gundog man is selling a trained dog to a novice handler! In fact, a good many men refuse to sell trained dogs, and their attitude is quite understandable. For the benefit of the uninitiated who contemplate buying a trained dog (if they can find one!) and for the harassed owner who is going to sell one. I offer the following advice.

The prospective purchaser, we will assume, has contacted a likely source of supply. He should request full details of the dog, including a copy of the pedigree, age, training and experience, temperament, etc. If all these particulars seem satisfactory, he should next endeavour to go and see the dog working for his present master. By doing this, much time and temper will be saved, and he can be assured of satisfaction. Failing this, he should depute an experienced friend to do so. It is strange that many men will cheerfuly pay £350 to £1000 for a trained dog, but grudge spending a few pounds on travelling to see him. This is very foolish, and may end in trouble for all concerned. If you see him working you can assure yourself that the dog is as stated, in which case you have secured a bargain, or that he leaves much to be desired, when you will have saved a lot of money!

Some advertisers will send a trained dog on trial, which in my opinion, is asking for trouble, and a practice in which I have never indulged. It is grossly unfair to all concerned, mostly to the dog himself, who usually has a long, tiring journey (perhaps the first in his life), is bundled out on to a platform, and in all probability taken out shooting the same day! Little wonder that trouble so often ensues. Nothing is calculated to upset a dog more than the combination of a train journey, strange surroundings, and a strange handler, with the result that he refuses either to hunt or to retrieve, and perhaps commits all sorts of heinous crimes. If you do have a dog down on trial, please give him a day or two to settle down and get used to you, and be sure that you know the correct words of command, whistles and signals. This may seem unnecessary advice, but it is extraordinary how often it is overlooked! Of course, it is up to the vendor to supply these details, but he, too, may lack previous experience of these very delicate transactions. Remember, too, that until a dog is completely used to, and happy in, his new home he will not give his best performance, and make due allowances; the type of country may also be different from that to which he has been accustomed.

We will next assume that the hypothetical deal has been concluded to the satisfaction, so far, of all concerned, excepting, perhaps, the dog, who naturally resents this violent upheaval in his ordered life. Here is my advice, and I can promise from actual experience that it is really sound:

(a) do everything possible to make the dog feel at home;
(b) feed and exercise him, as far as possible, in the same way as he has been used to;
(c) make allowances for his strangeness;
(d) do not work him until at least two weeks have elapsed since his arrival – longer if it seems advisable.

Try to see everything from the dog's point of view.

I need hardly add that if any perplexing incidents occur it is as well to get on to the previous owner of the dog as quickly as possible, and usually he can put you right. Few dogs reach maturity without developing one or two funny little mannerisms, about which the former master may have forgotten to tell you. It is very difficult to explain everything about your dog during the course of one conversation or a few letters – something is always sure to be overlooked.

The older the dog, the more set he will be in his ways, and the harder the task in getting him to work to your system. From the age of three years onwards this will be a difficult job indeed. Between one year and two a dog is more pliable – under a year very much more so. Few dogs are to be found trained under one year of age, and so the best age at which to buy a fully trained dog is from eighteen months to three years.

A final word of caution. If your new dog has previously lived in, and you intend him to live in a kennel, be patient at first. He will bark and howl, and (consideration for your neighbours notwithstanding) do not go and pacify him each time he howls or he will always do so in order to bring you to him. Do not beat him for his rowdiness or you will lose his confidence for ever and never get the best out of him at work.

I think I have set down the chief points to be borne in mind when buying a trained dog, and if both parties will only conduct themselves in a sportsmanlike manner and to be open with each other, neither should ever have cause to regret the deal.

THE SLACK HUNTER

The problem which sometimes faces the trainer, as well as the shooting man, is how to get a no-slip retriever to hunt. Often one sees advertised a dog which is just what one wants, but which has been trained only as a no-slip retriever.

I once undertook the training to hunt of a springer who had been trained by his keeper-breeder as a retriever pure and simple, and whose experience of hunting-up game was very limited indeed. This dog had had a good deal of experience upon partridges, and was used to collecting runners. His age was eighteen months or thereabouts.

As is usual in these cases, a rather longer time was required before the pupil was quite at home, but once I was satisfied that this was the case I took him out with the gun to see just what he could do. I found, in this case, that the dog would retrieve, quickly and to hand and would search industriously for a lost dummy or bird among light cover such as roots; in the woods, however, he was practically hopeless – would hardly leave heel, and even then would come in again at the slightest opportunity.

In the first place I tried the rabbit pen, wherein the dog showed interest in the rabbit, but his previous steadiness work had removed the desire to chase or even to push up, so I felt I was in for a hard task. With a dog of this description I think one is entitled to take a few liberties and to disregard a certain amount of unsteadiness – in fact one has almost to unsteady the dog in order to obtain the desired end.

Often it will be found that the example of a keen hunting dog will do the trick, but at first I must confess failure with my pupil, who did not care to follow his kennel-mate through the rough cover in search of scent. This I found to be most important – the non-hunting dog must be taken out for training to a place where there is scent and game in order to stimulate his interest; it is practically hopeless to try and teach hunting upon scentless ground.

After a few days of this treatment by example, I discontinued the use of another dog, and took Jas out on his own. A few pieces of meat thrown into promising cover had a certain good effect, care being taken that this treatment was carried out before feeding time when the dog was hungry. After a time, I struck lucky, and a piece of meat fell in cover within a few inches of a rabbit in his seat. The dog saw the rabbit, and remained steady, but I was pleased to notice that (after eating his meat) he sniffed interestedly at the vacant seat, and seemed inclined to follow the line of the lately departed rabbit. This I allowed him to do for, although a foot scent is not as a rule to be followed by a spaniel (who should seek a body scent), I was anxious to get my pupil hunting. Time enough to correct the technical faults when the dog is a keen hunter.

The next lesson I found that Jas sought the cover more eagerly, and without the aid of a meat lure. Another rabbit was disturbed, and this time I gave the command, 'seek 'em', the moment he was flushed. Off went the dog in full cry, but only for a short distance because the rabbit went into a thick pile of brushings. Into this bundled my dog, and out came the rabbit. I fired a blank, and the pupil half dropped, ran on, and then decided that discretion was the better part of valour and stopped. For this he received a great petting, and was immediately taken home, but later in the same evening taken out with a young bitch who hunts keenly, and whose example might now do a great deal of good. It did! Within a few moments they were both hunting well and Jas might have been at it all his life, though I noticed a distinct falling off of interest directly the scent grew weak. All that remained to be done was to steady him again, and to let time and experience teach him to hunt as eagerly where the scent is bad as where it is good – for what use is a spaniel which will not hunt unless there is fresh scent lying?

It may appear strange that a spaniel should ever require teaching to hunt; perhaps teaching is too strong a word – encouraging would be better. It must be remembered that, while hunting is an hereditary instinct, it is also an instinct which becomes to a certain extent dormant through lack of use, and no-slip training tends to encourage a dog to concentrate upon a blood scent instead of hunting a body scent. Judicious treatment is needed to bring out such a dog.

I may be censured by some for encouraging this dog to chase but, while I admit that the same end could probably have been gained without resorting to such a drastic method, it was imperative to hurry the dog on to hunting; his previous display of steadiness had convinced me that to bring him back to the path of virtue would not be an overly difficult task.

9

Kennels and ferreting

KENNELS AND DISINFECTING

The man who keeps his dog in a kennel has certain admitted advantages over the man whose dog lives in, and foremost among these advantages is the fact that the dog's quarters can be thoroughly disinfected and fumigated if disease should pay a visit. A correspondent recently told me that he had lost a puppy through mange, or rather had had one destroyed owing to the persistence of the disease, and that his vet had told him not to introduce another dog into the house for at least six weeks. Had the dog been lying in a kennel, the place could have been thoroughly fumigated with a sulphur candle and washed down with disinfectant.

One of the finest things for disinfecting a kennel is the old ARP stirrup pump used in conjunction with a good disinfectant, and no damage is caused to the pump if it is thoroughly cleaned out with fresh water afterwards. With a stirrup pump, every nook and cranny of the kennel can be reached by the disinfectant when the jet is used, and the spray is useful for swilling down the yard or run. Even if disease has not reared its ugly head, I consider that every kennel should be disinfected regularly in this manner, apart from the routine cleaning. Once a week in summer and about once a fortnight in winter is a good formula, and by this means disease may often be prevented and parasites kept under. In the case of a dog which constantly fouls his kennel, a more frequent washing out will be necessary. It should not be forgotten that after an attack of disease all the kennel equipment and utensils, collars, chains, leads, brushes, etc., should also be disinfected.

While on the subject of kennels, I have heard many theories

propounded in favour of this type or that, and the subject interests me greatly. We hear arguments in favour of wood, brick, concrete, asbestos and heaven knows what; one breeder prefers to keep his dogs in one big range, while others plump for the small group or sectional kennel system. I naturally have my own pet ideas, which, alas, have never been put into practice due to a lack of both opportunity and funds; suffice to say that I consider wood the most suitable type of flooring whenever possible, and that the sleeping accommodation should also be built of wood. Concrete I dislike, even as a floor for the runs (though I have been forced to use it for the sake of convenience, and recently of necessity), as I consider it may cause rheumatism owing to its damp, porous nature, and constant sitting upon it wears the dog's coat. For all this, it looks smart, is easily cleaned and disinfected, and is practically everlasting.

As for the kennel system, much as I like the idea of a large range under one roof, with the dogs divided according to sex and age into various compartments (with consequent advantages in bad weather, from the kennelman's point of view), this system has very grave disadvantages when disease comes; unless one has a complete spare range of kennels or can get rid of all the dogs for a few days, it makes a thorough fumigation impossible. On top of this separate breeding kennels will be necessary in any case, and also an isolation ward for any sick dogs; by the time the sick dog is detected and isolated, however, the chances are that every dog in the range will have been exposed to infection. If, on the other hand, the dogs are kennelled in little groups of three or four in separate kennels with runs, contact with the sick dog is down to a minimum. Incidentally, in my experience it seems almost impossible to completely isolate healthy dogs from infection, even if you have only one invalid, as the germs will be carried upon the kennelman's hands, clothes, boots and cleaning tools unless the most rigid disinfection is carried out each time the patient has been visited; knowing human nature as I do and realizing the impossibility of having a complete change of clothing several times a day over a long period, I am rather sceptical about this! Indeed, I often wonder how frequently a vet carries disease from one kennel to another.

Returning to the subject of kennels, I think that the system of scattered kennels, for want of a better term, has much to recommend it, even if it does mean a certain amount of discomfort when going from one to the other during winter. As regards runs, I am a little undecided whether these should be roofed or not. Certainly a roof means that the dogs can be out at exercise and play all the year round, in any weather, but as I am such a great believer in fresh air, sunshine and general hardiness both for human beings and dogs, I rather incline to the open run. After all, there are few days even in the worst winters when the dogs cannot be out for an hour or so at least, and in the summer great benefit is derived both by mature dogs and puppies from open air and sunshine, providing that a certain amount of shade is given. For some breeds, perhaps, the roofed run is essential, but for the hardier gundogs I should say that it is by no means so. The ideal run would, of course, be one with a sliding head which could be pushed back in summer and drawn forward in bad weather, but in my own case this is just one of the dreams of the future, which I have grave fears will never come true!

In any kennel, no matter what its type or construction, the things to avoid are draught, damp and overheating. For those who advocate or use a system of artificial heating I have nothing but contempt, and consider that they are doing their dogs a great injustice by making them unnecessarily pampered. One can carry modern refinements a little too far, and a dog that is not reasonably tough is not worth keeping, at any rate for sport. Ensure comfort and absence of draught and damp in your kennel, but do not make a hot-house flower of your dog, or you will live to regret it.

DOGS AND FERRETING

What of the man who does a lot of ferreting, and what sort of training must his general-purpose dog be given? This question sometimes crops up and, as there are few of us who do not have a day out with the ferret occasionally, it is natural that the dog must be what advertisers sometimes call broken to ferrets.

The main consideration, in my opinion, is to have the dog so well under control that he can (a) be seated at a distance from the burrows to be ferreted (and not in the direction in which the rabbits are likely to bolt); (b) stand seeing the ferret popping his head out of a hole, and even coming above ground and running about, without making a dive for him; and (c) be steady to bolted rabbits. Point (a) should be a foregone conclusion if the dog has been taught to drop at a distance and remain at the drop, and (c) will provide first-class training in steadiness. We are left with item (b) – steadiness to ferret, as it might be called.

Some people make a practice of housing their dogs in the same building as the ferret hutches, and no doubt this results in familiarity breeding contempt on the part of the dog. However, it is not a practice to be recommended and I much prefer to take my puppy out quietly with a tame and docile ferret, drop the puppy, and allow the ferret to run about close by. Each time the puppy shows undue interest in the movements of the ferret he must be checked, and should he make a dive for it he must be severely checked. A few lessons of this kind and the puppy will remain indifferent to the ferret; usually the ferret will treat the dog with equal indifference. Next, the ferret should be put down a few holes from which he is unlikely to bolt anything, and the puppy seated a few yards off in view of the burrows. Any attempt on the puppy's part to move when the ferret comes out must again be nipped in the bud immediately, and the dog pegged down if this appears to be necessary.

Silence is golden during ferreting operations, and a dog which will drop to signal or a low whistle scores heavily in this work. Indeed, I have known dogs who were so used to ferreting that they would automatically take up the most advantageous position without any orders, and remain steady throughout the whole proceedings until signalled to collect a dead or badly wounded rabbit. Many ferreters use dogs of the whippet, lurcher or terrier type, and these dogs are, of course, supposed to deal with any rabbits which escape the nets or appear to be getting away unwounded. These dogs specialize in this type of work, and a somewhat different technique is necessary for their training, as naturally they are not expected to be steady. It must not be thought that I am dealing with this; my remarks are intended purely for one who has an occasional day ferreting with his general-purpose dog and his gun.

I remember reading an article about a dog which was trained to 'retrieve' the ferret when he came above ground. If my memory serves me rightly, the dog would also plant the ferret down outside any hole indicated! This, of course, demonstrates very clever training of both dog and ferret, but I cannot see that it serves a very useful purpose, and is certainly not to be recommended to the average shooter.

When ferreting rabbits, one should, on the first few occasions, tie up the young dog if he is likely to exhibit any unsteadiness towards the bolting rabbits. A check cord can be used if the ferret is being handled by a companion, the dog and master taking up a position behind or above the burrows, though not in the line of fire (a seemingly unnecessary caution, perhaps, but one which I have known ignored!). A few days at this sort of thing and most dogs will remain dead steady to both bolting rabbits and the fall of shot rabbits. It is, in fact, one of the most valuable lessons in steadiness which can be given, always providing that there is someone other than the dog's master handling the ferret, and that the bag can be made subservient to dog training.

Some men prefer to do their ferreting without the company of a dog, but this is a mistake, because rabbits are liable to be wounded and get away, and many dogs become clever tellers at rabbit holes, indicating whether the burrow is occupied or not. This saves time and trouble, even if you are fortunate enough to possess a ferret which refuses to go down a vacant earth – an accomplishment which most clever ferrets acquire with experience. Some men recommend that cover adjacent to the burrows to be ferreted should be hunted through by the dog, with the object of putting the rabbits to ground. In my experience rabbits are very disinclined to bolt after being chased to ground by dogs, and more often than not the ferret kills below ground, and then there ensues either a long and tedious wait or some strenuous digging operations. Far better to hunt the dog after all the rabbits have been bolted, as a few have probably escaped and may be hiding in nearby cover.

Another precaution: do not send the dog to collect a dead or wounded rabbit until the ferret reappears and all the rabbits have been bolted from that particular earth; otherwise the dog may be accidentally shot while hidden by cover. This applies especially when ferreting in company. If, for humanitarian reasons, the dog must be dispatched immediately, any succeeding rabbits which bolt must not be fired at.

I see no earthly reason why the average general-purpose dog should not be the constant companion of his master on all shooting expeditions, and if this sort of work is given early, when the dog is trained but young enough to benefit from new experiences, he becomes wiser and wiser as time goes on and can be a real asset. The man who cannot take his spaniel or retriever ferreting because he makes such a nuisance of himself is missing a great deal of enjoyment, and is at the same time either an inefficient or a lazy trainer – or perhaps, both!

10

Between you and your dog

Relationship between master and dog is all important – it must be a *happy* relationship which, ideally, combines mutual love and respect. Canine psychology, as it has come to be called, requires that the master should try to think along the same lines as his dog, sort out the whys and wherefores of the animal's sometimes inexplicable behaviour, and treat it in a way that it understands.

This applies not only to matters of training and handling, but also to general management – housing, feeding, exercising and health questions. I am sorry to have to say this, but owners can be so blind and foolish in their treatment of their dogs that I sometimes marvel that we do not see many more mentally disturbed dogs, although, heaven knows, we see enough!

My strong feelings on this subject have motivated me to include this chapter of random jottings, in no particular order, dealing with some of these ifs and buts of gundog ownership, training and general management. They are not as comprehensive as I would have wished, and they are, in some cases, unavoidably overlapping and repetitive. However, I hope and believe that they will give the reader much food for thought, help to put him on the right lines in his thinking, and foster a happier relationship between him and his dog.

SPRINGTIME PROBLEMS

Springtime can be a trying period for dogs and owners alike, glorious though the season may be! It is not only the young man's fancy that lightly turns to thoughts of love, but also that of young (and old!) dogs. With the onset of warmer weather, bitches come into season and dogs start to roam in search of a mate, it is surprising how they seem to get the message that there is a receptive lady on their patch, or even some miles off it.

The question of sheep-worrying is one of my hardy annuals, and lambing time is a particularly dangerous period. Even the best behaved of dogs, if given too much freedom and the opportunity to gang up with its mates, can get itself and its owner into serious trouble by sheep-worrying because, even if it does not actually attack, injure or kill sheep, it may well cause ewes to abort simply by chasing them. Little wonder that so many irate farmers, with every justification, reach for their shotguns to protect their valuable flocks. While it seems to me that the majority of country-dwelling gundog owners are aware of their responsibilities, those living on the edge of towns are often very lax and seem completely unaware of how easily and quickly their dogs can get into the fields and into mischief. I see examples of it almost daily in my district.

Skin troubles – and skin vermin – erupt very suddenly and violently in the spring, especially if the weather suddenly turns mild. Eczema, in both wet and dry form, is pretty common, especially in some strains of certain breeds (notably golden retrievers) of gundog, and I always advocate that this should receive immediate veterinary attention. It may be a bloodstream infection or due to an allergy, is often caused by incorrect feeding and failure to pay attention to cleanliness in the kennels, and can prove difficult to clear up. Much simpler to deal with, once diagnosed, are the burrowing mites which cause sarcoptic mange and also the more common surface parasites such as fleas and lice. All these respond very quickly to treatment with one of the modern powders or washes, which usually contain gammexane in one form or another.

Routine worming treatment is advisable at this time of the year, and as most animals, like humans, are physically at their lowest ebb after the winter, the introduction of a vitamin and mineral supplement into the diet may prove very beneficial. I am something of a vitamin fanatic (especially for myself!) and feel quite certain that my very quick recovery from a bout of 'flu was largely the result of a course of vitamins and minerals. However good we may believe our diet to be, these days so much of our food has been processed, frozen and otherwise devitalized and denaturalized that, from time to time, a vitamin and mineral supplement is probably very necessary.

Most, if not all, of the modern, pelleted, all-in type of dog food have already been supplemented with vitamins, minerals and amino acids. Certainly the one I use, Skinner's Dog Food, has these additives and has proved most satisfactory over the seven years I have been feeding it to the entire kennels. Even so, if a dog becomes below par, or enters the kennels in a poor physical condition, I have no hestitation in supplementing its diet still further by the use of the proprietary vitamin-mineral Canovel, or something similar, which can be obtained from veterinary surgeons or veterinary chemists. This type of product is also very useful for bitches in whelp and lactating, and for weaned puppies.

Whilst on the subject of dry all-in dog foods, it might be helpful to stress that, where these are used, the dog *must* at all times have free access to water, because the moisture content of the food is so low (something under eight per cent in most cases). Another point that I have discovered is that the few owners who have complained that their dogs scour on the food are invariably *overfeeding* them. One of the most difficult facts to get over to owners – and to ladies in particular – is that the diet is concentrated and low in water content, so that the prescribed amount fed *looks* quite inadequate by ordinary standards! Fed on the recommended basis, this type of food will, in at least ninety-five per cent of cases, be acceptable to, and relished by, the consumer, and will result in firm and normal stools being passed. A blessing to kennelman and householder alike!

PUPPY SELECTION

One of the most frequent – and the most difficult to answer! – questions hurled at me concerns the choice of a puppy from a litter of, say, eight to twelve weeks of age. If there is a short answer, it is to ignore any pups which have obvious physical or mental defects, and then go 'eeny, meeny, miny, mo' among the remainder! Few, if any, of our experienced breeders and trainers will claim to be able to choose the right one every time, even though they may have an eye for a dog. It is far easier for a show fancier to pick a puppy at such a tender age than it is for we folk who are mainly concerned with working ability and temperament.

Over the years, gallons of ink must have been spilled on this subject, every expert coming up with his own ideas and suggestions, none of which is infallible. Anyone who has bred and reared a litter of gundog puppies will tell you that individuals change from day to day, or at any rate from week to week, and today's pick of the litter may easily become an also-ran tomorrow. Shy pups can become bold pups almost overnight, and vice versa; the runt may well outgrow its brethren within a few weeks, while the non-retriever or the cover-shy specimen can change its attitude very quickly indeed, especially when it receives personal attention as a one-and-only and ceases to be a member of a group.

Joe Greatorex once advised me that the only reasonably certain way of selecting a working puppy from a litter was to run the whole lot on until they were six to ten months of age and had started training, and that, even then, you could be wrong! Which is not much consolation to the one-dog man who, by force of circumstances, must make a spot decision when interviewing a litter of pups at the breeder's kennels. Picking a working gundog puppy at an early age is at best a chancy business, but far less chancy if you go to a breeder with a reputation to maintain, and you are satisfied that *the puppies really are bred from genuine working stock.*

I have often been lucky in my choice of puppy either by picking the one which nobody else wanted, the smallest of the litter, or by relying upon my wife's feminine intuition. I happen to like the more sensitive type of dog which needs encouragement rather than repression, because I have almost invariably discovered that these (with careful treatment and handling) make the best mature workers *for me.* Some of my colleagues prefer tough dogs, and so seek boldness and a degree of extroversion displayed at an early age. I certainly always have a weakness for the puppy which really looks at me, even if it is a bit diffident about sudden movements and loud noises, so long as it is not obviously a nervous wreck. But I always look at *both ends* of the pup under consideration.

However, I recognize the fact that I am in a very different position to the average one-dog owner, who has neither the time, facilities nor expertise to deal with too many early problems. He (especially if he is a complete novice) is probably best advised to choose a puppy which is reasonably bold and confident, and which he (and his wife!) like the look of and feel they can cope with. I repeat previously offered advice to such folk – if in doubt, take along to the selection session a friend of greater experience, and note his suggestions. If really experienced, he will leave you in no doubt that even he *could* be wrong and that he will not be prepared to carry the can if his choice does not come up to your expectations! Remember that a puppy of eight weeks is just a baby, and who in this world can predict just how a baby will turn out in adult life?

DEFEATISM

I can never understand the defeatist attitude adopted by so many inexperienced gundog owners regarding travel sickness in their animals. Time and again I hear of dogs which have to be left at home if a shoot is more than a few miles away, and others which have to be so sedated with travel-sickness pills before the journey that they are virtually useless for at least the first half of the day.

The trouble almost invariably arises because the owners do not accustom the dog to travelling from an early age. Indeed, quite a few never even consider taking the puppy out in the car until the shooting season comes round by which time the pup is (or should be) pretty well mature. On the other hand, I know of owners who have tried their pups in the car at an early age and then, because they were sick, failed to persevere.

An additional cause of travel sickness is the mistaken practice of feeding the dog shortly before the journey. This, of course, is asking for trouble, and is quite unnecessary. Indeed, a dog should not be expected to work on a full stomach although you can, if you are worried about its energy requirements, safely give it a tablespoonful of honey (neat or dissolved in a little water or milk). Indeed, this is recommended by some authorities to prevent car-sickness.

It must be admitted that there is a small proportion – very small – of dogs which never become acclimatized to travelling by car, no matter how early they are introduced to it and despite all the usual dodges of earthing the car chassis by trailing a wire or chain to prevent static electricity building up, ensuring adequate ventilation, and obscuring view. The vast majority of dogs, however, will come to love travelling if they are properly handled from puppyhood, shown that the car is nothing to fear and encouraged by being fed in the stationary vehicle). In my experience, once a dog has learned that a journey is likely to end in what it loves most of all – free running exercise and work – your troubles are over. I cannot stress too forcibly the necessity for perseverance during the early days, even if this does entail various unpleasant and smelly mopping-up operations and a certain amount of discomfort for other passengers on a few occasions. All worthwhile, surely, to ensure that you have a dog that you can take anywhere, on shooting days or for holidays.

TEMPERAMENT – HUMAN AND CANINE

Open any book on gundog training and, somewhere or other, you will read about the importance of the pupil's temperament and the bearing that it will have upon your educational efforts. Some authors stress that the temperament of the *trainer* is also a vital factor in the attainment of a satisfactory end product, and that ideally the two must really click. This is all very well for the man who has a kennel full of puppies from which to choose, and who has also come to know himself, but the ordinary one-dog owner, especially if a novice, is probably stuck with whatever puppy he buys and, most certainly, his own ability, patience and understanding of the canine mind is an unknown quantity!

We dog writers – forgive the Americanism! – can (and often do) pontificate until we are blue in the face about choosing the right dog and then thinking like a dog, but we are still bombarded with queries from readers who, quite obviously, failed to achieve such utopia either because they thought they knew it all before they started with their puppy, or because they have failed to mark, learn and inwardly digest the pearls of wisdom which dropped from our typewriters! However, for all that, we must face the fact that, no matter how well-bred a puppy may be, you can still end up with a wrong 'un, and that by no means every owner is capable of training and handling even the most trainable of dogs simply because he has not got the temperament for the job. The wonder to me is that, with all the human and canine frailties which abound, the success rate of the average novice owner is so high. Not only this, but it is increasing all the time, as can be witnessed on almost any shoot and at field trials and tests. So perhaps we are not knocking our heads against a brick wall, after all!

Any trainer who has had many dogs through his hands will tell you that he just cannot get on with certain animals, for no definable reason. A few weeks ago I was chatting to one of our leading professionals who has more than once won the championship stake for his particular breed. He told me that at least two of his champions were dogs to which he would not have given kennel room had they not belonged to valuable clients, but because they did he just had to do his best with them and finally won through. My friend is a remarkably astute trainer with a temperament quite ideal for the job, and one of the exceptions which proves the rule. Other professionals of my acquaintance, both past and present, have been far less patient with their pupils (or their clients, for that matter!) and speedily rejected dogs which, although possessing obvious potential, were not their cup of tea. I have never been able to *make* myself like a dog if it was not my sort and, once at odds with it, I would find that I was getting nowhere fast and, worse still, building up a defeatist attitude towards the dog and finding all sorts of excuses not to take it out. However, the same dog, passed over to an assistant or a colleague, often made the grade, several even proving positively brilliant in their work and a credit to their handler.

Patience is always held up as being an essential requirement in a gundog trainer and, to a certain extent, this is true. But, on the other hand, I know several brilliant trainers who are anything but patient, but succeed because they have the knack of picking the type of dog which clicks with their own personality and temperament. One of the most efficient semi-professional spaniel trainers I know is a man whose patience with human beings is almost non-existent. Not only will he not suffer fools gladly, but he can become quite violent if thwarted; yet with dogs he really has what it takes, and seems capable of bringing out the best in the most unlikely specimens.

Some handlers like hard dogs. Others, myself included, do better with softer animals who require encouragement rather than repression during training. For some quite indefinable reason, I have always found myself more on the same wavelength of shy and somewhat introverted dogs which require bringing out, and have usually found them to be the most successful mature workers. Whether or not this is because I was a shy and introverted child (something which my friends find hard to believe!)

I do not know, but it is a fact. Many of my more forceful colleagues completely despise this type of dog, and tend to reject it out of hand.

Dogs vary in temperament just as much as human beings do, and the ordinary owner who picks a young puppy from a litter is, quite literally, in the lap of the gods. He may end up with the right animal, or he can be at odds with it before the end of a week. The chances are that, if his wife and family have any say in the matter, he is stuck with it and has got to do his best to make a worthwhile shooting companion of it, come what may. If he likes it right from the start, the prognosis is favourable. If he does not, he must be extra careful to study not only the pup's temperament but his own as well, and bend over backwards to get the two to harmonize and make a reasonable job of training. So long as the dislike is not mutual, there is always hope, and the owner who really has the will to win through and can regard the whole business of canine education as a challenge – especially if he is open-minded and holds no strongly preconceived ideas on the subject – stands at least a fifty-fifty chance of ultimate success.

THOUGHTS ON FEEDING

One of the most interesting aspects of my life, for more years than I care to remember, has been meeting other gundog folk and visiting the kennels of my colleagues, discussing training problems and learning the many and various ideas that they hold about everything concerning dogs, from breeding to general kennel management and feeding. It is, truly, quite astounding how systems and techniques vary from kennel to kennel, and almost all appear to be successful as regards the end product, however much they differ!

I can well understand the novice gundog owner-handler becoming completely confused if, as I so often suggest, he picks the brains of his more experienced contemporaries in order to gain knowledge of the subject. I most certainly did when I started up with gundogs, and even the books by experts which I read offered very conflicting advice on many points. However, over the years I evolved my own system and ideas – quite how I do not know but probably through picking out what I considered to be the soundest advice and that which suited my circumstances and somewhat peculiar temperament.

Nowadays, more amateurs than ever are breeding dogs, some for the interest of it and some in the hope of making a little profit on the side. There are those – the fortunate few – to whom the economics of the hobby mean little or nothing, while others have just got to be realistic in their approach and at least break even in the financial sense. The proliferation of dogfoods on the market is quite bewildering, every manufacturer claiming that his product is the best, be it canned, frozen, fresh meat, or all-in pellets or meal.

At one time or another I have experimented with almost everything that dogs can eat and during the war years it was amazing how well my kennel inmates did on the most unlikely mixtures when I was forced to use whatever was available. For instance, for one period of about four months their diet consisted almost entirely of boiled potatoes, dried blood and bone meal, plus cod liver oil, without any dire results. What little biscuit or meal that could be obtained then was made from white flour which had been subjected to the agenizing process, and this was found to cause hysteria, especially in young puppies, a very serious and worrying condition which today is almost unknown.

As soon as it was available again, I changed back to feeding raw meat and offal, especially sheeps' paunches and bullocks' tripes, which I still hold to be a very sound and acceptable diet for dogs *if you can afford it* or for that matter even *obtain* it. Unfortunately, the market has been ruined for the small-scale user by manufacturers of canned and frozen dogfood and prices have gone sky high, with abbatoirs reluctant to sell meat in small quantities anyway. The alternatives are 'knacker's' meat (which must by law be sold cooked), frozen meats of various kinds, canned dogfood, fresh butcher's meat (for human consumption), which is expensive, or one of the many all-in pelleted or meal products. The field is wide open, but the practical kennelman (or ordinary dog owner, for that matter) must consider such important points as suitability, acceptability, convenience and economy of the food he gives to his stock.

The dedicated owner and breeder will, doubtless, experiment with the different types of food, just as I did, and arrive at his own conclusions. From time to time he will be swayed by the glowing advertisements in the media which extol the virtues and economy of this product or that, or be influenced by personal advice proffered by friends or writers like myself. The great thing is to find, and stick to, a form of feeding which suits your dogs, your circumstances and your pocket. In my own case, after very careful trials and experimentation, I have come down wholeheartedly on the side of dry all-in feeding, using pelleted food for adults, and meal, supplied *ad lib* in a hopper, for lactating bitches and young puppies. The latter require all the sleep they can get, and hopper feeding at weaning time prevents unnecessary disturbance, as well as allowing them to eat *what they want when they want it*, thus preventing them from gorging themselves as they are liable to do if given meals at set hours. It also has the distinct advantage of allowing the breeder to get out for a few hours, or even a whole day, without worrying about getting back to feed the pups, or arranging for someone else to do so. This is quite a consideration, because I have found a lot of people make a rod for their own backs in this respect, some even refusing to entertain the idea of a litter of puppies 'because they are such a tie'!

VERSATILITY

> *What has been said concerning the valuable qualities of nose which are implanted by hunting for game, brings up the question whether retrievers proper are justifiably forbidden all access to this advantage. And the answer must be that there is no reason whatsoever why the retriever of genuine hunting instinct – and you cannot make a good worker out of the other sort – should not be allowed to hunt for his master. As in the case of the spaniel,* everything depends upon the ingraining beforehand of steadiness and obedience. *When these habits have become second nature the retriever may be sent out to seek game in likely pieces of holding covert, and according to how he conducts himself the experiment may be extended or diversified. Just as the retriever which has never been allowed to gather fur is liable to outbreaks of unsteadiness, so the animal which has never hunted game under the eye of his master has less reason to remember that when a rabbit breaks across his path his share in the proceedings is, for the time being, a passive one.*

Thus wrote the late Dick Sharpe in his book, *Dog Training by Amateurs*, first published in 1924, and I quote him for the benefit of those readers whose shooting calls for a questing dog but who are dubious about utilizing a retriever rather than a specialist spaniel, even though their preference lies with the former. Like myself, Dick Sharpe had learned that most men will make a better job of a dog of a breed they really like, even if its suitability for the particular type of work is questionable, than of one to which, for some quite indefinable reason, they cannot take.

For all that, I know from my conversations with him that Dick Sharpe was fully aware of the limitations of retrievers as questing dogs, just as he was of those of spaniels used for driven-game shooting and, if asked a straight question, he would recommend 'the horse for the course'. However, he saw nothing wrong in making a gundog, of any breed, as versatile as possible – indeed, he positively encouraged it, but never missed an opportunity of emphasizing, again and again, the fact known to all trainers of experience, that everything depends upon the preliminary course and 'the ingraining beforehand of steadiness and obedience'.

Let there be no doubt about it: it is in this aspect of gundog training that the average owner-handler tends to slip up, especially the novices, and query after query which I receive from readers demonstrates this most forcibly. They are in so much of a hurry to get their dogs on to the interesting and practical shooting work that they only give them a perfunctory course of hand training, never really getting completely on top of their pupils even in unexciting conditions; then they complain that the dogs go completely haywire and commit every crime in the book when taken out into the shooting field among live game and, very often, in company.

Sometimes, in gundog training, it seems that you just cannot win! I write this because I have seen quite a few beginners (and also some of the older hands, for that matter, myself included!) go to the other extreme, and so overdo the early discipline lessons that they get their pupils wooden and sticky, inhibit their enthusiasm and drive and even, occasionally, eradicate their style. Some start their pups too early, others overdo the lesson periods both in length and intensiveness, and others still are altogether too aggressive and/or tend to credit their pupils with far more understanding than they actually possess. All of which boils down to the desirability of getting to know, not only your pupil, but yourself as well. Considering how intensive most of us are about canine psychology, the wonder to me is that so many novice trainers achieve the excellent results that they do and, without any shadow of doubt, the standard is improving all the time, as is witnessed by the ever-increasing number of successes gained at field trials by genuinely amateur owner-handlers over the last few seasons.

When using a gundog for a type of work for which it was not specifically intended, the handler must not only ensure that the preliminary obedience training is thorough, but also, in the most tactful manner possible, inhibit those natural instincts which are inimical to that work. For example, retrievers love to range far and wide, and are not natural 'weavers' in a prescribed pattern, as spaniels are. Therefore, if they are to be used as questers, they must, from the commencement of their education, be conditioned to working within gunshot range of their handlers. Again, retrievers are not such natural lovers of thick cover as are the questing breeds, and this aspect of their work must also receive early priority.

In the same way, spaniels which are intended for use as no-slip retrievers on driven game must, very early on, be taught patience and given artificial experience to this end, and not be allowed to become too keen on questing unshot game, which is their natural scene. Sitting still for long periods is anathema to spaniels, as is ranging close to the handler for retrievers, so in both cases the trainer is having to inhibit the deep-rooted instincts of his pupil.

The up-and-coming pointer-retriever breeds appear to be very versatile in both respects and, while it cannot be claimed for them that they quest, or deal with cover, with the same *technique* as a spaniel, they are capable of waiting patiently at a drive without making a nuisance of themselves, and can usually be trained to quarter within reasonable gunshot range when required, even though their natural pointer tendencies are to take in a large area of country in their casts. It is, undoubtedly, this versatility which accounts for their increasing popularity with the new generation of shooting folk who seek an all-rounder (and, preferably, one of medium size and with a short coat, so important to houseproud wives!). But even if we have the complete answer, we shall still have those who wish to train retrievers as questers and spaniels as formal shooting dogs!

IMPROVISATION

One of the musts in a retrieving or questing gundog (with the exception of pointers and setters used for their traditional work) is courage when facing thick and thorny cover, whether or not the dog is aware that the cover contains game, shot or unshot. Thankfully, most of our genuine working strains of gundog more especially the spaniel breeds, have a natural penchant for facing thick cover but even these may prove reluctant to thrash it out unless and until they have been given quite a bit of specific experience of brambles, briars and blackthorn, and have, by the association of ideas, learned that therein may lurk their natural quarry.

Many and various are suggestions of experts about encouraging youngsters to deal with cover. Some advocate stomach appeal, and advise the handler to cast biscuits, pieces of meat or, indeed, anything edible into cover of increasing degrees of thickness, in order to encourage confidence. Others like myself, try to avoid this particular reward system unless all else fails, and prefer to rely upon tactful use of the retrieving dummy, the example of a cover-loving 'schoolmaster' or the presence of natural game (or game *scent*) to give their puppies the right idea, quite early on in the training programme.

Almost all the systems have their advantages and disadvantages, like practically every other aspect of canine education. One must always experiment and try to discover the most suitable approach for the disposition of the particular pupil. I like to get my puppies out into cover as early as possible, starting off in thick grass and gradually working up to really difficult stuff. This can be done by taking them for country walks and by tactful use of the retrieving dummy with, perhaps, the example of an experienced dog (the dam is, of course, ideal) as well. However, crafty pups will soon learn that they can safely leave hunting cover to their mentor, and will simply sit outside it waiting for something to be flushed – and, in all probability, chased!

When there were plenty of rabbits about, not only laying attractive scents but also making easy entrance to the thickest of bramble patches, it was comparatively easy to encourage even the most backward of pupils to hunt cover, at any time of the year. Nowadays, most of us have to improvise conditions, unless (as in my own case) the rabbit situation is improving. One enthusiastic friend of mine has been most successful in this respect by using his loaf and his hutch rabbit. First of all he makes artificial runs-in in patches of cover, runs the rabbit through them to lay a scent trail, and drops among them a rabbitskin dummy, which has been rubbed against the rabbit's rear to give an attractive scent! As soon as the rabbit has been caught and boxed up, the puppy is brought out and encouraged to hunt the area. Quite a lot of work is entailed, obviously, but the system definitely works, and has proved to be very worth while. Incidentally, as the pup's education progresses, the same rabbit is used for early steadiness lessons with equal success, and has survived five seasons, to my knowledge, without harm.

Another friend used brailed pheasants in much the same way, when training his young retrievers to face cover, but found homing pigeons, wing-clipped, equally effective, far cheaper to keep and more convenient to transport. Quite a lot of trainers use live pigeons in traps, arranging their training course along similar lines to that seen in gundog tests at gamefairs and similar events. The birds are released by 'remote control', a string is pulled by the handler or his assistant as the dog reaches the traps; thus a natural find and flush is simulated. If nothing else, gundog training teaches the handler the value of improvisation, and the necessity to anticipate the actions of the pupil and, at all times, to keep one jump ahead. Once the penny has dropped and a dog realizes that cover holds the game, or game scent, in which he delights, he will forget all about pricks and scratches, and drive in and thrash about with gusto – which is the whole object of the exercise.

MAJOR FAILINGS IN OWNERS

Over the years I have discovered three major failings in many dog owners. These are: (a) crediting the dog with a reasoning power which it does not possess; (b) lack of consistency and positiveness in handling; and (c) failure to grasp the fundamental principles of canine nutrition and general management. The vast majority of the queries which I receive fall into one or more of these categories and, when they are carefully explained, my answers are generally understood, appreciated and acted upon with, I am pleased to say, usually beneficial results.

Much of the improvement I have noted in the handling and management of dogs is, undoubtedly, due to the fact that the canine world in general, and the gundog section in particular, is extremely well catered for as regards literature, and the proliferation of books on every aspect of a dog's life has been very marked over the last ten years or so. Each of the major, and many of the minor, breeds has one or more specialist books entirely devoted to it, while gundogs of every type are covered by training books galore. Nowadays, there is no excuse for anyone to say, 'I did not know'.

It matters not what breed of dog you own, or for what purpose you keep it; *the vital thing is to get to know your dog and understand its temperament* (which varies as much in canines as in human beings), *and to appreciate its limitations of intelligence and reasoning power.* Forgive me for saying so, but owners can be so stupid, especially in respect of the handling and general management of their dogs. As an example, let me quote one common and oft-repeated complaint: that the dog (because the owners have failed to provide it with a kennel and run wherein it can be put when not under supervision) goes off roaming and not only provides a hazard on the road but gets into all sorts of mischief, from dustbin scrounging to poultry- or sheep-worrying. 'I gave him a good hiding when he came home,' says the owner, 'but it didn't do any good. The next time he stopped away all night, and wouldn't even come in when I found him in the garden in the morning.'

The reason the good hiding did not do any good, and the dog was reluctant to come in on the next occasion, was purely and simply because it connected its owner's violence with the very last action it made, which was coming home. Animals only learn by the association of ideas, and if you really wish to stop your dog roaming then the time to chastise it is when it is *in the act of wandering off*. It would have been far better to make a great fuss of the dog and give it a good meal upon its return! The best way to make a dog stop away from home all night is to beat it on its return. Canine psychology is not all that difficult to understand, once you appreciate the way dogs tick and their almost complete lack of reasoning power. You have to *show* a dog where it is wrong, and correct it at the right time and in the right place.

I believe it was the late Colonel G. H. Badcock who wrote that there is no such thing as over-training, only *bad* training, and I suppose he would have said much the same thing about undertraining! I believe that the art of training a gundog – or any dog for that matter – is knowing how far to go and just when to stop, coupled with an accurate assessment not only of the pupil's temperament and capacity to absorb education, but also the disposition of the trainer himself. Most novice trainers – and quite a few experienced ones as well! – are over-impatient, and try to force the pace and cut corners with their pupils. They tend to start intensive training far too early, but fail to observe the danger signals of lassitude, boredom, even stickiness – such as sitting to command but refusing to come when called – which their puppy may display.

This trouble is exacerbated by making training periods too long, and by conducting them in the wrong climatic conditions, such as on very hot, humid days when scenting is poor or even non-existent, or on cold, wet ground. This particularly applies to the early, repetitive hand-training exercises and general obedience work.

Dogs react to over-handling in different ways. The shy, sensitive and somewhat inhibited character becomes wooden and sticky, as mentioned above, while the bold, boisterous extrovert does the exact opposite, takes the bit between his teeth and becomes so fed up with commands and discipline that he closes his ears and treats the handler as though he did not exist, deaf to voice and whistle, completely unrepentant, and seemingly impervious to any form of chastisement!

The latter symptoms, of course, are also displayed by dogs which have been *under*-trained, and it is often difficult for the casual observer to differentiate between the two and to put his finger on the exact trouble! However, the under-trained dog can generally be spotted because the handler is obviously not its main centre of interest; it does not look at him nor watch his movements. It also tends to respond to simple obedience commands in a slovenly fashion, wriggle about when put on the drop, and retrieve and deliver in a careless fashion.

Gundog trainers should lean over backwards to keep the balance, in order to end up with a dog which goes with drive, enthusiasm and style but it is at all times under complete control: difficult, but by no means impossible, to achieve, given the desire to learn, the ability to think like a dog, and a great deal of patience, plus – and this is most important – a pupil of the right breeding.

Another facet of training, which ties up nicely with that under discussion, is the handling technique, particularly in regard to the two Ns, noise and nagging! Our best handlers direct their dogs with the minimum of fuss and noise, vocal or whistled; when they do give a command, however, by whatever means, it is immediately understood and obeyed. Although I would not go so far as to say that the noisy handler is necessarily a bad handler, it is an undoubted fact that much more is achieved from a dog if you are gentle and quiet, meaning what you say and saying what you mean to it. The nagging type of trainer keeps on nattering at his dog without being definite enough in his meaning, with the result that it becomes so used to a sort of running commentary on its performance, minus any action, that it ends up regarding the trainer's efforts as incidental music and ignores them completely, thus, I feel sure, losing a great deal of respect for his owner. In my book, it is essential for dog and master to hold each other not only in mutual affection, *but also in respect*, and this will only be achieved by *consistent and positive* handling from the start.

The age at which a gundog puppy should commence its intensive training course is a question I am frequently asked about and is of great importance. Most training manuals are vague on the subject, the usual recommendation being that around six months of age is the best time to start. However, so much depends upon the temperament of the puppy, and probably even more upon that of the trainer, that this suggestion cannot be more than a generalization, and should be accepted as such. Nowadays, most professional trainers of both spaniel and retrievers find that the average pupil is not really ready to absorb *intensive* education until it is eight, nine or even ten months of age, even though some of the preliminaries of basic good behaviour can be instilled at an earlier age.

The amateur owner-trainer is not limited, timewise, as is the professional, and he should plan accordingly. The easy-going placid and patient handler, given a puppy of a fairly bold disposition can make an earlier start than the more impetuous trainer, while *anyone* finding themselves having to deal with a shy, sensitive or inhibited puppy should delay commencing the main course until the dog is old enough to take it – all the more so if the trainer himself is lacking in patience and self-control. If in doubt, always err on the side of caution, and feel your way. Whatever the temperament of the puppy you are going to train, do not make the mistake of giving it too much latitude and freedom, such as allowing it to roam the district at will and indulge in hunting alone and like misdemeanours, for to permit this is to court disaster and probably to prevent yourself ever gaining complete control over your pupil. Far better to kennel the dog strictly when it is not actually in the company of a responsible member of the household, thus making it happy to be taken out and all the more receptive to education.

Retrieving problems crop up nearly as frequently as steadiness problems, and create quite a lot of headaches for novice owner-trainers. It is no secret that I have strong feelings about forcing a dog to retrieve, in the belief that what we all want is a *natural* retriever, which picks up and carries because it loves doing so, and not because it has been pressurized. Like breeds like; natural retrievers breed natural retrievers. I fear that unless we are firm over this question we shall soon get to the stage where the majority of puppies require forcing, which would be highly undesirable for the average owner-trainer since the technique is intricate, time-consuming, and certainly no task for the novice.

Most trainers, like myself, are discovering that more and more puppies coming into kennels are reluctant retrievers, and call for very specialized treatment. By no means all these, however, require forcing, but need only encouragement and experimentation to bring out the dormant natural delight in retrieving. The first step is to discover something which the dog is pleased to pick up and carry, and to use this, initially, to get the message over. In his book *Gundog Training by Amateurs*, the late Dick Sharpe quoted the case of a non-retrieving cocker which was receiving its final brushing before being dispatched for sale by auction:

> *When I happened to lay down the brush, Jack promptly picked it up and rushed off to his kennel. By way of experiment I followed him and relieved him of the brush, patting him as I did so, the while fondling the brush in a tantalizing manner. Then I threw it out of the kennel door, and Jack at once retrieved it. We then adjourned to the field, and no matter where the brush was thrown it was promptly fetched. After that no better or keener retriever could be imagined and great expectations were formed; but alas, before they had time to materialize, distemper claimed him!*

I might add here that I have myself found that most puppies will happily retrieve the grooming brush, unattractive though it might appear to us. Even disinterested adults can become quite interested and not only in grooming brushes, at that!

Dick Sharpe recommended that the trainer of an unpromising pupil

> *must always be ready to visualize some incident in childhood which may account for unwillingness to retrieve. For instance, what could be more simple than for* [*a puppy*] *to have seized and run away with a slipper, to have been chided for the liberty and ever after to have avoided such misbehaviour? . . . to bridge the gap between retrieving a brush and refusing to retrieve* [*a*] *stuffed stocking,* [*enclose the brush*] *in a stocking, so imparting to the object which had been viewed with disfavour the choice aromas of the brush.*

Brushes are by no means the only unlikely objects a dog may take to retrieving. You can, indeed, try anything bar the kitchen sink, so long as the dog likes it and it can be thrown, carried, and subsequently cased in a stocking, skin, cloth or canvas to be used as a dummy. Once retrieving this has become second nature and is properly performed, there will usually be no trouble in achieving an equally satisfactory response with other dummies and, ultimately, the real thing. The time and trouble entailed in this sort of experimentation are, I am convinced, far preferable to working on, or paying for, a course of force retrieving and, if successful, gives the owner a tremendous glow of satisfaction as a bonus!

The check cord has its uses, but can very easily be abused, and dogs quickly learn to behave when it is worn and riot when it is off! It should only be used as a last resort when all other attempts to control fail, and usually proves most valuable with difficult and recalcitrant pupils

Steadiness in the poultry-run helps to lay the foundations to future discipline in the shooting field

Waiting at the kennel door for permission to enter – valuable practice in general obedience . . .

. . . as is patience at feeding time

Dogs which are inclined to be travel-sick can be encouraged to accept the car by being fed therein, thus associating it with something pleasant

A useful type of outdoor kennel for one or two dogs

Potential workers – a litter of ten English Springer pups, aged seven weeks, in the car for the first time

The author – a lifelong roughshooter

Conclusion

'MORE FLIES WITH HONEY . . .'

I believe that every book should have a succinct conclusion, and I have been racking my brains for an apt quotation applicable to the art of gundog training and handling. Suddenly I remembered one of the many pearls of wisdom that dropped from the lips of one of my oldest friends and mentors, a man who taught me a lot about nature, wildlife and gundogs, Don Thompson, onetime headkeeper on the Bourne Estate, near Canterbury. 'You will catch more flies with honey than you will with vinegar,' he used to tell me.

How true this is! I have applied the dictum time and time again, when dealing with difficult and recalcitrant dogs, nervy specimens and those which suffered from mental blocks or had, somehow or another, got hold of completely the wrong idea. Just another way, I suppose, of saying, 'Softly, softly, catchee monkey.'

There are times, I know only too well, when it is difficult, if not impossible, to keep your temper when handling a dog, and I am the last person to advocate being *too* soft. However, I have almost invariably discovered that, when things go wrong during a dog's schooling, the honeyed approach is far more effective than the big stick.

So, if you keep this in mind, and endeavour to see things from the dog's point of view, you stand a good chance of succeeding in your efforts and, above all, in obtaining and retaining, not only the love, but also the respect of your pupil. Unless you can establish this mutual respect and *rapport*, all your work will be wasted and you can forget about the whole business. I am conceited enough to believe that if you read, absorb and act upon the advice contained in this book, such will not be the case. Good luck.

APPENDIX A

Glossary of terms

Blind Retrieve: The collection of a retrieve which the dog has not marked.

Check Cord: A long cord on the same principle as the lead, for use when the dog is working at a distance during early training.

Choke (Check) Lead: A short lead with a ring or D at one end and a hand-loop at the other. The loop end is slipped through the ring, forming a choke, which goes round the dog's neck and acts as a collar, tightening or slackening easily according to pull of the dog.

Dropping to Shot: Sitting or lying immediately upon the sound of gunfire.

Dummy: Object of soft material, for teaching a dog to retrieve before introduction to real game.

Dummy-launcher: An adaption of the well-known 'beer can' target launcher, this ejects a special dummy by the firing of a .22 blank cartridge. Useful for early and advanced retrieving lessons, teaching a dog to mark, and accustoming it to the sound of gunfire.

Flushing: Putting up game.

Hard Mouth: The damage of game by a dog while it is retrieving.

Line: The scent trail left by a bird or animal.

Marking: Watching the fall of the dummy or a bird and going straight to it with accuracy.

No-slip Retriever: A dog which walks to heel lead-free and retrieves as required, but it is not used for questing for unshot game.

Pegging: The catching of live and unwounded game and animals.

Pointing: Indication of the presence and scent of game by the dog stiffening, with extended muzzle and tail, and sometimes one forefoot raised.

Questing (Hunting): Searching for game in front, and to either side, of the handler.

Runner: A wounded bird or animal which has moved on.

Running in: Moving forward to chase or retrieve without being ordered to do so by the handler.

Towered Birds: A bird is said to have 'towered' when, after being shot, it flies on for some distance apparently untouched, and then rises vertically and plummets to earth, stone dead. This is thought to be due to the bird having been shot in the lungs, and it is usually found lying on its back after falling.

Working to Hand: The ability to accept signalled directions.

APPENDIX B

Organizations holding gundog training classes and/or working tests

BRISTOL AND WEST WORKING GUNDOG SOCIETY: R. Davis, Fairlawn, Back of Kingsdown Parade, Cotham, Bristol 6. (Retrievers and spaniels)

CHILTERN GUNDOG TRAINING CLUB: Mrs June Barry, Beacons Bottom, Stokenchurch, Buckinghamshire. (Retrievers and spaniels)

CLWYD RETRIEVER CLUB: Mrs G. Bailey, Gunstock Kennels, Whitford, Holywell, Clwyd. (Retrievers)

DUKERIES (NOTTS) GUNDOG CLUB: Mrs R. Davies, The Paddocks, Clumber Park, Worksop, Nottinghamshire. (Retrievers and spaniels)

EAST MIDLAND GUNDOG TRAINING CLUB: Mrs M. Nixon, The Old Rectory, Rectory Lane, Nailstone, Nuneaton, Warwickshire. (Retrievers and spaniels)

ESSEX SPANIEL GET-TOGETHER: J. Ford, Hill Cottage, Chancers Lane, Fordham, Colchester, Essex

FORTH AND CLYDE WORKING GUNDOG ASSOCIATION: Mrs M. Paton, 2 Kilncraigs Road, Alloa, Clackmannanshire Scotland. (Retrievers and Spaniels)

GERMAN SHORTHAIRED POINTER ASSOCIATION: H. Fisher, Firhouse, 32 Cherry Lane, Lawton Heath End, Alsager, Stoke-on-Trent, Staffordshire. (Pointer-retrievers)

GERMAN SHORTHAIRED POINTER CLUB (MID-ANGLIAN GROUP): C. P. Snelling, 4 The Street, Euston, Thetford, Norfolk. (Pointer-retrievers)

HIGHLAND GUNDOG CLUB: M. Smith, Norleigh Gundog Kennels, Drybridge, Buckie, Banffshire, Scotland. (Retrievers and spaniels)

IRISH WATER SPANIEL ASSOCIATION: Mrs J. W. Johnson, 77 Russell Road, Horsell, Woking, Surrey. (Irish water spaniels)

KENNET VALLEY GUNDOG TRAINING SOCIETY: Mrs E. Henbest, Talltrees, Rag Hill, Aldermaston, Reading, Berkshire. (Retrievers and spaniels)

KENT, SURREY AND SUSSEX LABRADOR RETRIEVER CLUB: Mrs V. Markham, Jayflight Kennels, Stansted, Sevenoaks, Kent (Retrievers).

MIDLANDS SPANIEL GET-TOGETHER: Mrs R. Cockrill, Brookfield Lodge, Hackman's Gate Lane, Belbroughton, Worcestershire. (Spaniels)

MID-SUSSEX WORKING SPANIEL AND TRAINING CLUB: Mrs G. Newbury, 27 Balaclava Road, Surbiton, Surrey. (Spaniels)

NORFOLK GUNDOG CLUB: B. G. Colman, 6 Cedar Close, Downham Market, Norfolk. (Retrievers and spaniels)

NORTHERN GOLDEN RETRIEVER ASSOCIATION (PENNINE TRAINING AREA): Mrs S. Buckley, Intake Head, Delph, Oldham, Lancashire. (Any variety gundog)

SUFFOLK GUNDOG TRAINING CLUB: F. E. Steel, Garden House, Newbourn, Woodbridge, Suffolk

THREE SHIRES SPANIEL MEET: Mrs Boon, 7 George Street West, Macclesfield, Cheshire. (Spaniels)

UNITED GUNDOG BREEDERS ASSOCIATION: R. Moseley, Laburnum Cottage, Woodseaves, Staffordshire. (Retrievers and spaniels)

UNITED RETRIEVER CLUB (Retrievers)

Border Counties and Cotswolds: Mrs D. Philpott, School House, Cranham, Gloucester.

Buckinghamshire: I. P. Dalrymple, 13 Tomlins Close, Tadley, Basingstoke, Hampshire.

Essex: B. G. Ellis, 87 Stock Road, Billericay, Essex.

Hampshire: B. G. Hall, Crowhurst Boarding Kennels, Sutton Wood Lane, Bighton, Alresford, Hampshire.

Lincolnshire: Miss I. Osborne, West Torrington Grange, Wragby, Lincolnshire.

Midlands: F. Ellis, 4 Cavendish Drive, Kidderminster, Worcestershire.

North Midlands: Mrs A. Forster, Higher Hardings Farm, Higher Sutton, Macclesfield, Cheshire.

Southern: E. Rowlands, 11 London Road, Southborough, Tunbridge Wells, Kent.

WELSH SPRINGER SPANIEL CLUB: Mrs A. Lewis, Sunnymede. Longwick Road, Princess Risborough, Buckinghamshire, (Welsh springer spaniels)

WESTWARD GUNDOG SOCIETY: Mrs M. Curgenven, Keepers Lodge, Burlescombe, Tiverton, Devon. (Retrievers and spaniels)

Index